NEW YORK NOTARY PUBLIC STUDY GUIDE WITH 5 PRACTICE EXAM

ALL-IN-ONE PREP BOOK INCLUDES:

FULL SUMMARIZATION OF ALL SECTIONS

200 PRACTICE QUESTIONS

50+ BONUS QUESTIONS

BOLTON ❦ PREP

Copyright © 2024 by Foundry Direct

ALL RIGHTS RESERVED. By purchase of this book, you have been licensed one copy for personal use only. No part of this work may be reproduced, redistributed, or used in any form or by any means without prior written permission of the publisher and copyright owner.

Foundry Direct is not affiliated with or endorsed by any testing organization and does not own or claim ownership of any trademarks. All test names (and their acronyms) are trademarks of their respective owners. This preparation book is for general information and does not claim endorsement by any third party.

This publication is designed to provide accurate and authoritative information regarding the subject matter covered. It is distributed with the understanding that the publisher, authors, or editors are not engaged in rendering legal or another professional service. If legal advice or other expert assistance is required, the services of a competent professional should be sought.

Foundry Direct is not legally liable for any mistakes, omissions, or inaccuracies in the content of this publication. Foundry Direct does not guarantee that the user of this publication will pass the exam or achieve a level of performance. Individual performance on the exam depends on many factors, including but not limited to the level of preparation, aptitude, and individual performance on test day.

Printed in the United States of America.

TABLE OF CONTENTS

INTRODUCTION i
PROFESSIONAL CONDUCT 1
   APPOINTMENT AND QUALIFICATIONS 4
   POWERS AND DUTIES 16
   RESTRICTIONS AND VIOLATIONS 47
DEFINITIONS AND GENERAL TERMS 77
SCHEDULE OF FEES 85
TEST-TAKING STRATEGIES 86
PRACTICE TESTS 88
   PRACTICE TEST 1 90
   PRACTICE TEST 1: ANSWER KEY 95
   PRACTICE TEST 2 99
   PRACTICE TEST 2: ANSWER KEY 104
   PRACTICE TEST 3 107
   PRACTICE TEST 3: ANSWER KEY 112
   PRACTICE TEST 4 115
   PRACTICE TEST 4: ANSWER KEY 120
   PRACTICE TEST 5 123
   PRACTICE TEST 5: ANSWER KEY 128
TRUE OR FALSE: ANSWER KEY 130

INTRODUCTION

Congratulations on taking the first step towards becoming a notary public in the state of New York. This comprehensive guide is your key to success in the New York Notary Exam. Crafted by seasoned professionals well-versed in notary public laws, this book is the result of meticulous analysis of past exam papers. By identifying the crucial elements that correlate with exam success, we've distilled the laws and regulations governing these questions into easily digestible outlines.

We aim is to demystify the complex world of notary public laws, statutes, and legal jargon. We've gone the extra mile to present this information in an unofficial yet simplified manner, making it accessible to all readers. After each section, you'll have the opportunity to test your understanding with true or false questions, reinforcing your knowledge.

After thoroughly absorbing the content in each chapter, you'll be well-prepared to tackle the seven practice tests, comprising a total of 200 multiple-choice questions. These tests will be your invaluable companions on your path to success. We strongly recommend taking your time between each practice test, and thoroughly reviewing your answers to ensure you absorb the material effectively.

It's important to note that this book is designed as a valuable companion to the official NYS Division of Licensing Services booklet, Notary Public Licensing Law. For the most comprehensive preparation, we strongly recommend reading both resources in tandem. Together, they will equip you to confidently tackle and conquer the New York Notary Exam.

The New York notary public license law booklet can be found on the official New York State Department of State website:
https://dos.ny.gov/notary-public

Note

Where gender pronouns appear in this booklet, they are meant to refer to male, female, non-gendered, and nonbinary persons.

BECOME A NOTARY PUBLIC IN NEW YORK

Every New York notary public applicant must meet the following requirements.

You must:
- Be at least 18 years old
- Be a person of good moral character
- Reside within the state or maintain a business office in New York
- Have the equivalent of a "common school education"
- Be a U.S. citizen or legal permanent resident
- Complete the application process
- Not be convicted of a crime unless the Secretary of State finds that the crime committed doesn't bar you from commission

As long as all the requirements are met, you are eligible to take the 1-hour New York State notary exam. There are 40 multiple-choice questions on the exam and the applicant must correctly answer at least 70% of the questions to pass.

What to Bring for the Exam:
- Bring a non-expired government-issued photo ID
- $15 exam fee (check, money order, or credit card only)
- Two #2 pencils. Pencils will not be provided at the exam site

Exam results will be mailed as a "pass slip" once the results are available; typically, within 4-6 weeks. If you passed the exam, congratulations! Complete the state application and include the $60 application fee and the original pass slip. The state application can be found on the Division of Licensing Services section of the New York State Department of State website: https://dos.ny.gov/licensing-services

PROFESSIONAL CONDUCT

Use of the office of notary in other than the specific, step-by-step procedure required is viewed as a serious offense by the Secretary of State. The practice of taking acknowledgments and affidavits over the telephone, or otherwise, without the actual, personal appearance of the individual making the acknowledgment or affidavit before the officiating notary, is illegal.

The attention of all notaries public is called to the following judicial declarations concerning such misconduct:
"The court again wishes to express its condemnation of the acts of notaries taking acknowledgments or affidavits without the presence of the party whose acknowledgment is taken for the affiant, and that it will treat serious professional misconduct the act of any notary thus violating his official duty." (Matter of Napolis, 169 App. Div. 469, 472.)

"Upon the faith of these acknowledgments rests the title of real property, and the only security to such titles is the fidelity with which notaries and commissioners of deeds perform their duty in requiring the appearance of parties to such instruments before them and always refusing to execute a certificate unless the parties are actually known to them or the identity of the parties executing the instruments is satisfactorily proved." (Matter of Gottheim, 153 App. Div. 779, 782.)

Equally unacceptable to the Secretary of State is slipshod administration of oaths. **The simplest form in which an oath may be lawfully administered is:**
"**Do you solemnly swear that the contents of this affidavit subscribed by you is correct and true?**" (Bookman v. City of New York, 200 N.Y. 53, 56.)

Alternatively, the following affirmation may be used for persons who conscientiously decline taking an oath. This affirmation is legally equivalent to an oath and is just as binding:
"**Do you solemnly, sincerely and truly declare and affirm that the statements made by you are true and correct?**"

Whatever the form adopted, it must be in the presence of an officer authorized to administer it, and it must be an unequivocal and present act by which the affiant consciously takes upon himself the obligation of an oath. (Idem, citing People ex rel. Kenyon v. Sutherland, 81 N.Y. 1; O'Reilly v. People, 86 N.Y. 154, 158, 161.)

Unless a lawyer, the notary public may not engage directly or indirectly in the practice of law. Listed below are some of the activities involving the practice of law which are prohibited, and which subject the notary public to removal from office by the Secretary of State, and possible imprisonment, fine or both. A notary:

1. **May not give advice on the law.** The notary may not draw any kind of legal papers, such as wills, deeds, bills of sale, mortgages, chattel mortgages, contracts, leases, offers, options, incorporation papers, releases, mechanics liens, power of attorney, complaints and all legal pleadings, papers in summary proceedings to evict a tenant, or in bankruptcy, affidavits, or any papers which our courts have said are legal documents or papers.
2. **May not ask for and get legal** business to send to a lawyer or lawyers with whom he has any business connection or from whom he receives any money or other consideration for sending the business.
3. **May not divide or agree to divide** his fees with a lawyer, or accept any part of a lawyer's fee on any legal business.
4. **May not advertise in, or circulate** in any manner, any paper or advertisement, or say to anyone that he has any powers or rights not given to the notary by the laws under which the notary was appointed.

A notary public is cautioned not to execute an acknowledgment of the execution of a will. Such acknowledgment cannot be deemed equivalent to an attestation clause accompanying a will.

SUMMARY

The New York Secretary of State views deviations from notary procedures as serious offenses. Notaries must not take acknowledgments or affidavits without the physical presence of the person involved. Engaging in such practices is illegal.

Courts condemn the practice of notaries acknowledging or attesting documents without the actual presence of the parties involved. Such actions are deemed as professional misconduct, undermining the integrity of legal documents and real property titles.

Notaries are required to administer oaths or affirmations in person. The law specifies simple forms for oaths and equivalent affirmations for those who object to taking oaths. The process must be a conscious act in the presence of an authorized officer. The simplest form to administrate an oath is the following:

"Do you solemnly swear that the contents of this affidavit subscribed by you is correct and true?"

Notaries who are not lawyers are prohibited from practicing law. This includes preparing legal documents, giving legal advice, soliciting legal business, sharing fees with lawyers, or claiming legal powers beyond those granted by law.

Notaries are advised against acknowledging the execution of wills, as this does not equate to an attestation clause required for wills.

Notaries may face removal from office, imprisonment, fines, or all for engaging in prohibited practices or failing to adhere to the required procedures and standards set by the Secretary of State.

TRUE OR FALSE?

1. A New York notary public is allowed to take acknowledgments or affidavits over the telephone if the person is not physically present.

✓ Answer key on Page 130

APPOINTMENT AND QUALIFICATIONS

Appointment and Qualifications		
Law	Section	Subject
Executive Law	130	Appointment of Notaries Public
Executive Law	131	Procedure of Appointment; Fees
Executive Law	132	Certificates of Official Character
Executive Law	133	Certification of Notarial Signatures
Executive Law	140	Commissioner of Deeds, NYC
Election Law	3-200	Commissioner of Elections
	3-400	
Public Officers Law	3	Qualifications for Holding Office
County Law	534	County Clerk; Appointment of Notaries
Miscellaneous		Member of Legislature
Miscellaneous		Sheriffs
Miscellaneous		Disqualifications

EXECUTIVE LAW

Section 130 - Appointment of Notaries Public

1. The Secretary of State may appoint and commission as many notaries public for the State of New York as in his or her judgment may be deemed best, whose jurisdiction shall be co-extensive with the boundaries of the state.

The appointment of a notary public shall be for a term of 4 years.

An application for an appointment as notary public shall be in form and set forth such matters as the Secretary of State shall prescribe. Every person appointed as notary public must, at the time of his or her appointment, be a resident of the State of New York or have an office or place of business in New York State.

A notary public who is a resident of the State and who moves out of the state but still maintains a place of business or an office in New York State does not vacate his or her office as a notary public.

A notary public who is a nonresident and who ceases to have an office or place of business in this state, vacates his or her office as a notary public.

A notary public who is a resident of New York State and moves out of the state and who does not retain an office or place of business in this State shall vacate his or her office as a notary public.

A non-resident who accepts the office of notary public in this State thereby appoints the Secretary of State as the person upon whom process can be served on his or her behalf.

Before issuing to any applicant a commission as notary public, unless he or she be an attorney and counselor at law duly admitted to practice in this state or a court clerk of the Unified Court System who has been appointed to such position after taking a Civil Service promotional examination in the court clerk series of titles, the Secretary of State shall satisfy himself or herself that the applicant is of good moral character, has the equivalent of a common school education and is familiar with the duties and responsibilities of a notary public; provided, however, that where a notary public applies, before the expiration of his or her term, for reappointment with the county clerk or where a person whose term as notary public shall have expired applies within 6 months thereafter for reappointment as a notary public with the county clerk, such qualifying requirements may be waived by the Secretary of State, and further, where an application for reappointment is filed with the county clerk after the expiration of the aforementioned renewal period by a person who failed or was unable to re-apply by reason of his or her induction or enlistment in the armed forces of the United

States, such qualifying requirements may also be waived by the Secretary of State, provided such application for reappointment is made within a period of 1 year after the military discharge of the applicant under conditions other than dishonorable.

In any case, the appointment or reappointment of any applicant is in the discretion of the Secretary of State. The Secretary of State may suspend or remove from office, for misconduct, any notary public appointed by him or her but no such removal shall be made unless the person who is sought to be removed shall have been served with a copy of the charges against him or her and have an opportunity of being heard. No person shall be appointed as a notary public under this article who has been convicted, in this State or any other state or territory, of a crime, unless the secretary makes a finding in conformance with all applicable statutory requirements, including those contained in article twenty-three-A of the correction law, that such convictions do not constitute a bar to appointment.

2. A person regularly admitted to practice as an attorney and counselor in the courts of record of this state, whose office for the practice of law is within the State, may be appointed a notary public and retain his office as such notary public although he resides in or removes to an adjoining state. For the purpose of this and the following sections of this article such person shall be deemed a resident of the county where he maintains such office.

SUMMARY

In New York, the Secretary of State has the authority to appoint and commission an unspecified number of notaries public, whose authority extends across the entire state. These appointments last for four years. To qualify, applicants must either reside in New York or maintain an office or business within the state at the time of appointment. If a resident notary moves out of state but keeps a New York office, they remain a notary; however, nonresidents who no longer have an office or business in the state, or residents who leave without maintaining a business presence, must relinquish their notary position.

Non-residents who become notaries are required to designate the Secretary of State as their agent for service of process. The Secretary must ensure that applicants, except certain exempt professionals like attorneys and court clerks, are of good moral character, have at least a common school education, and understand a notary's duties. Exemptions to these requirements may be granted under specific circumstances, such as reappointment application before term expiration, military service, or within six months to one year after military discharge.

The Secretary has the discretion to appoint, reappoint, suspend, or remove notaries for misconduct, provided the accused can respond to the charges. Convicted individuals can be appointed only if their crimes are deemed not to bar their appointment as per relevant laws.

Attorneys with a practice in New York who live in adjoining states can also be appointed as notaries and are considered residents of the county where their office is located.

TRUE OR FALSE?

2. A notary public who does not practice law may retain their appointment upon moving out of state if they intend to return.

✓ Answer key on Page 130

Section 131 - Procedure of appointment; fees and commissions

1. Applicants for a notary public commission shall submit to the Secretary of State with their application the oath of office, duly executed before any person authorized to administer an oath, together with their signature.

2. Upon being satisfied of the competency and good character of applicants for appointment as notaries public, the Secretary of State shall issue a commission to such persons; and the official signature of the applicants and the oath of office filed with such applications shall take effect.

3. The Secretary of State shall receive a non-refundable application fee of $60 from applicants for appointment, which fee shall be submitted together with the application. No further fee shall be paid for the issuance of the commission.

4. A notary public identification card indicating the appointee's name, address, county and commission term shall be transmitted to the appointee.

5. The commission, duly dated, and a certified copy or the original of the oath of office and the official signature, and $20 apportioned from the application fee shall be transmitted by the Secretary of State to the county clerk in which the appointee resides by the 10th day of the following month.

6. The county clerk shall make a proper index of commissions and official signatures transmitted to that office by the Secretary of State pursuant to the provisions of this section.

7. Applicants for reappointment of a notary public commission shall submit to the county clerk with their application the oath of office, duly executed before any person authorized to administer an oath, together with their signature.

8. Upon being satisfied of the completeness of the application for reappointment, the county clerk shall issue a commission to such persons; and the official signature of the applicants and the oath of office filed with such applications shall take effect.

9. The county clerk shall receive a non-refundable application fee of $60 from each applicant for reappointment, which fee shall be submitted together with the application. No further fee shall be paid for the issuance of the commission.

10. The commission, duly dated, and a certified or original copy of the application, and $40 apportioned from the application fee plus interest as may be required by statute shall be transmitted by the county clerk to the Secretary of State by the 10th day of the following month.

11. The Secretary of State shall make a proper record of commissions transmitted to that office by the county clerk pursuant to the provisions of this section.

12. Except for changes made in an application for reappointment, the Secretary of State shall receive a non-refundable fee of $10 for changing the name or address of a notary public.

13. The Secretary of State may issue a duplicate identification card to a notary public for one lost, destroyed or damaged upon application therefor on a form prescribed by the Secretary of State and upon payment of a non-refundable fee of $10. Each such duplicate identification card shall have the word "duplicate" stamped across the face thereof, and shall bear the same number as the one it replaces.

SUMMARY

1. New York notary public applicants must submit their application, including an executed oath of office and their signature, to the Secretary of State.

2. Upon verifying the applicant's competency and character, the Secretary of State issues a commission that becomes effective along with the submitted oath and signature.

3. Applicants are required to pay a non-refundable $60 fee with their application, with no additional charge for the commission issuance.

4. A notary public ID card displaying the appointee's details and commission term is sent to the new notary.

5. The Secretary of State forwards the commission, oath, signature, and part of the application fee to the appointee's county clerk.

6. The county clerk indexes the received commissions and signatures for official records.

7. For reappointment, notaries must submit a new oath of office and signature to the county clerk.

8. The county clerk, upon completing the application review, reissues the commission, which then takes effect.

9. A non-refundable reappointment fee of $60 is collected by the county clerk, with no extra charge for the commission.

10. The county clerk sends the commission, application copy, and apportioned fee plus interest to the Secretary of State.

11. The Secretary of State records commissions received from the county clerk.

12. For changes in name or address, the Secretary of State charges a $10 non-refundable fee.

13. A duplicate ID card can be issued for a lost, destroyed, or damaged original for a $10 non-refundable fee, marked as "duplicate" and bearing the same number as the original.

TRUE OR FALSE?

3. A notary public is allowed one replace ID card free of charge.

✓ Answer key on Page 130

Section 132 - Certificates of official character of notaries public

The Secretary of State or the county clerk of the county in which the commission of a notary public is filed may certify to the official character of such notary public and any notary public may file his autograph signature and a certificate of official character in the office of any county clerk of any county in the State and in any register's office in any county having a register and thereafter such county clerk may certify as to the official character of such notary public.

The Secretary of State shall collect for each certificate of official character issued by him the sum of one dollar. The county clerk and register of any county with whom a certificate of official character has been filed shall collect for filing the same the sum of one dollar. For each certificate of official character issued, with seal attached, by any county clerk, the sum of one dollar shall be collected by him.

SUMMARY

The Secretary of State or the county clerk where a notary public's commission is recorded is authorized to certify the notary's official status. A notary public can file their signature and a certificate of official character with any county clerk across New York State or with a register's office in counties that have one. Once filed, the county clerk can certify the notary's official character.

For issuing each certificate of official character, the Secretary of State charges a fee of one dollar. Additionally, when such a certificate is filed, the county clerk and register will also collect a $1 filing fee. If a county clerk issues a certificate of official character with a seal, they will collect a fee of one dollar for it.

TRUE OR FALSE?

4. A notary public can file his signature and certificate of character in any county of the State he is commissioned in.

✓ Answer key on Page 130

Section 133 - Certification of notarial signatures

The county clerk of a county in whose office any notary public has qualified or has filed his autograph signature and a certificate of his official character, shall, when so requested and upon payment of a fee of $3 affix to any certificate of proof or acknowledgment or oath signed by such notary anywhere in the State of New York, a certificate under his hand and seal, stating that a commission or a certificate of his official character with his autograph signature has been filed in his office, and that he was at the time of taking such proof or acknowledgment or oath duly authorized to take the same; that he is well acquainted with the handwriting of such notary public or has compared the signature on the certificate of proof or acknowledgment or oath with the autograph signature deposited in his office by such notary public and believes that the signature is genuine.

An instrument with such certificate of authentication of the county clerk affixed thereto shall be entitled to be read in evidence or to be recorded in any of the counties of this State in respect to which a certificate of a county clerk may be necessary for either purpose.

SUMMARY

A county clerk whose office a notary public has filed his signature or has qualified, shall when requested and upon payment of $3, affix to any certificate, acknowledgment, or oath signed by the notary public in NYS, certify that the notaries public commission or certificate of character has been filed in his office and that he was authorized to take such proof, acknowledgment or oath; that he is well acquainted with the handwriting of the notary public or has compared his signature to that on file and believes in genuine.

An instrument with such certificate of authentication by the county clerk shall be read in evidence or be recorded in any county of NYS of which a certificate of a county clerk is required.

TRUE OR FALSE?

5. The county clerk can verify that a certificate of a notary has been filed and matches a signed document.

✓ Answer key on Page 130

Section 140 - Executive Law

14. No person who has been removed from office as a commissioner of deeds for the City of New York, as hereinbefore provided, shall thereafter be eligible again to be appointed as such commissioner nor, shall he be eligible thereafter to appoint to the office of notary public.

15. Any person who has been removed from office as aforesaid, who shall, after knowledge of such removal, sign or execute any instrument as a commissioner of deeds or notary public shall be deemed guilty of a misdemeanor.

SUMMARY

1. No person who has been removed from office as a commissioner of deeds for the City of New York is no longer eligible to be appointed again as a commission or as a notary.

2. Any person who has been removed from office as aforesaid, who shall, after knowledge of such removal, sign or execute any instrument as a commissioner of deeds or notary public shall be deemed guilty of a misdemeanor.

TRUE OR FALSE?

6. A person removed from office as a commissioner of deeds can be appointed a notary public following their probation.

✓ Answer key on Page 130

Section 3-200 and 3-400 - Election Law

A commissioner of elections or inspector of elections is eligible for the office of notary public.

SUMMARY

A Commissioner or inspector of elections is eligible to become a notary public.

TRUE OR FALSE?

7. An inspector of elections is eligible to become a notary public.

✓ Answer key on Page 130

Section 3 - Public Officers Law

No person is eligible for the office of notary public who has been convicted of a violation of the selective draft act of the U.S. enacted May 18, 1917, or the acts amendatory or supplemental thereto, or of the federal selective training and service act of 1940 or the acts amendatory thereof or supplemental thereto.

SUMMARY

Any individual who has been convicted under the Selective Draft Act of the United States, enacted on May 18, 1917, its amendatory or supplemental acts, or the Federal Selective Training and Service Act of 1940 and its amendments or supplements, is not eligible to hold the office of notary public in the state. This ensures that notaries public maintain a standard of conduct in alignment with federal and state legal expectations.

TRUE OR FALSE?

8. Violating the selective draft act automatically disqualifies a person from being a notary public.

✓ Answer key on Page 130

Section 534 - County Law

Each county clerk shall designate from among the members of his or her staff at least one notary public to be available to notarize documents for the public in each county clerk's office during normal business hours free of charge. Each individual appointed by the county clerk to be a notary public pursuant to this section shall be exempt from the examination fee and application fee required by Section 131 of the Executive Law.

SUMMARY

Each county clerk will have at least one notary public staff member available to notarize documents for the public during normal business hours free of charge.

Each staff member appointed to be a notary public is exempt from the examination fee and application fee.

TRUE OR FALSE?

9. There are no exemptions on who has to pay the fee to become a notary public.

✓ Answer key on Page 130

MISCELLANEOUS

Member of legislature

"If a member of the legislature be *** appointed to any office, civil *** under the government *** the State of New York *** his or her acceptance thereof shall vacate his or her seat in the legislature, providing, however, that a member of the legislature may be appointed *** to any office in which he or she shall receive no compensation." (§7 of Article III of the Constitution of the State of New York.) A member of the legislature may be appointed a notary public in view of transfer of power of such appointment from the governor and senate to the Secretary of State. (1927, Op. Atty. Gen. 97.)

SUMMARY

A member of the New York legislature must vacate their legislative seat if they accept any paid civil office under the state government. However, they are allowed to be appointed to a position where they receive no compensation. This includes the role of a notary public, especially since the authority to appoint notaries has been transferred from the governor and senate to the Secretary of State.

TRUE OR FALSE?

10. A member of the New York legislature can retain their seat in the legislature if they are appointed to a compensated civil office under the State of New York.

✓ Answer key on Page 130

Sheriffs

*** Sheriffs shall hold no other office. *** (§13(a) of Article XIII of the Constitution of the State of New York.)

SUMMARY
Individuals serving as sheriffs in the State of New York are prohibited from holding any other public office.

Notary public - disqualifications

Though a person may be eligible to hold the office of notary the person may be disqualified to act in certain cases by reason of having an interest in the case. To state the rule broadly: if the notary is a party to or directly and pecuniarily interested in the transaction, the person is not capable of acting in that case.

For example, a notary who is a grantee or mortgagee in a conveyance or mortgage is disqualified to take the acknowledgment of the grantor or mortgagor; likewise a notary who is a trustee in a deed of trust; and, of course, a notary who is the grantor could not take his own acknowledgment.

A notary beneficially interested in the conveyance by way of being secured thereby is not competent to take the acknowledgment of the instrument. In New York the courts have held an acknowledgment taken by a person financially or beneficially interested in a party to conveyance or instrument of which it is a part to be a nullity; and that the acknowledgment of an assignment of a mortgage before one of the assignees is a nullity; and that an acknowledgment by one of the incorporators of the other incorporators who signed a certificate was of no legal effect.

SUMMARY

A notary public may be ineligible to act in certain cases.

If a notary public is a party to or has a direct interest in the transaction, they are not able to act in that case.

For example, a notary who is the grantor, could not take his own acknowledgment.

If a notary is financially benefited or otherwise benefited from the conveyance, then the acknowledgment is nullified.

TRUE OR FALSE?

11. A notary public in New York may take acknowledgments in transactions where they have a direct financial or beneficial interest.

✓ Answer key on Page 130

POWERS AND DUTIES

Powers and Duties		
Executive Law	134	Signature and Seal of County Clerk
Executive Law	135	Powers and Duties
Executive Law	135-a	Acting Without Appointment, Fraud in Office
Executive Law	135-b	Advertising by notaries public
Executive Law	135-c	Electronic notarization
Executive Law	136	Notarial Fees
Executive Law	137	Statement as to authority
Executive Law	138	Powers of Notaries - Corporations
Executive Law	142-a	Validity of facts
Real Property Law	290	Definitions
Real Property Law	298	Acknowledgments and Proofs within the State
Real Property Law	302	Acknowledgments and Proofs By Married Women
Real Property Law	303	Requisites of Acknowledgments
Real Property Law	304	Proof by Subscribing Witness
Real Property Law	306	Certificate of Acknowledgment or Proof
Real Property Law	309-a	Uniform forms of certificates of acknowledgment or proof within this state
Real Property Law	309-b	Uniform forms of certificates of acknowledgment or proof without this state
Real Property Law	330	Officers Guilty of Malfeasance
Real Property Law	333	When Conveyances Not to Be Recorded
Banking Law	335	Unpaid Rental of Safe Deposit Box
Civil Practice Law and Rules	3113	Taking of Deposition by Notary
Domestic Relation	11	No Authority to Solemnize Marriage
Public Officers	10	Administering Oath of Public Officer

16 | NEW YORK NOTARY PUBLIC STUDY GUIDE

EXECUTIVE LAW

Section 134 - Signature and seal of county clerk

The signature and seal of a county clerk, upon a certificate of official character of a notary public or the signature of a county clerk upon a certificate of authentication of the signature and acts of a notary public or commissioner of deeds, may be a facsimile, printed, stamped, photographed or engraved thereon.

SUMMARY

The signature and seal of a county clerk, upon an official character certificate or a certificate of authentication of a notary public, may be facsimile, printed, stamped, photographed, or engraved.

TRUE OR FALSE?

12. The seal of a county clerk on an official character certificate of a notary public must be stamped.

✓ Answer key on Page 130

Section 135 - Powers and duties; in general; of notaries public who are attorneys at law

Every notary public duly qualified is hereby authorized and empowered within and throughout the State to administer oaths and affirmations, to take affidavits and depositions, to receive and certify acknowledgments or proof of deeds, mortgages and powers of attorney and other instruments in writing; to demand acceptance or payment of foreign and inland bills of exchange, promissory notes and obligations in writing, and to protest the same for non-acceptance or non-payment, as the case may require, and, for use in another jurisdiction, to exercise such other powers and duties as by the laws of nations and according to commercial usage, or by the laws of any other government or country may be exercised and performed by notaries public, provided that when exercising such powers he shall set forth the name of such other jurisdiction.

A notary public who is an attorney at law regularly admitted to practice in this State may, in his discretion, administer an oath or affirmation to or take the affidavit or acknowledgment of his client in respect of any matter, claim, action or proceeding.

For any misconduct by a notary public in the performance of any of his powers such notary public shall be liable to the parties injured for all damages sustained by them.

A notary public shall not, directly or indirectly, demand or receive for the protest for the non-payment of any note, or for the non-acceptance or non-payment of any bill of exchange, check or draft and giving the requisite notices and certificates of such protest, including his notarial seal, if affixed thereto, any greater fee or reward than 75 cents for such protest, and 10 cents for each notice, not exceeding five, on any bill or note.

Every notary public having a seal shall, except as otherwise provided, and when requested, affix his seal to such protest free of expense.

SUMMARY

Notaries public have the authority to carry out a broad range of official acts. These include administering oaths and affirmations, taking affidavits and depositions, certifying the authenticity of deeds, mortgages, and other written instruments, and demanding payment for or protesting non-acceptance or non-payment of bills and notes. Additionally, they can perform any duties permitted to notaries public by international law or laws of other jurisdictions, as long as they specify the name of the jurisdiction where such acts are to be used.

Attorney notaries may, at their discretion, administer oaths or affirmations to their clients, or take their affidavits or acknowledgments regarding any matter or proceeding.

Notaries are liable for any damages caused by misconduct in the execution of their duties. They are also restricted in the fees they can charge: a maximum of 75 cents for protesting non-payment of a bill or note, and 10 cents for each notice related to the protest, up to a maximum of five notices.

Finally, when requested and where applicable, notaries must affix their seal to a protest without charging extra.

TRUE OR FALSE?

13. A notary public is authorized to take affidavits and depositions in the State of New York.

✓ Answer key on Page 130

Section 135-a - Notary public or commissioner of deeds; acting without appointment; fraud in office

1. Any person who holds himself out to the public as being entitled to act as a notary public or commissioner of deeds, or who assumes, uses or advertises the title of notary public or commissioner of deeds, or equivalent terms in any language, in such a manner as to convey the impression that he is a notary public or commissioner of deeds without having first been appointed as notary public or commissioner of deeds, or

2. A notary public or commissioner of deeds, who in the exercise of the powers, or in the performance of the duties of such office shall practice any fraud or deceit, the punishment for which is not otherwise provided for by this act, shall be guilty of a misdemeanor.

SUMMARY

1. It is illegal for anyone to present themselves as a notary public or commissioner of deeds without being duly appointed to such positions. This includes holding out to the public through any means, such as advertising or using the title in a way that suggests they hold the office when they do not.

2. Any appointed notary public or commissioner of deeds found to be practicing fraud or deceit during the execution of their duties, for which no specific penalty has been outlined in the act, will be charged with a misdemeanor.

TRUE OR FALSE?

14. A notary public committing fraud has committed a felony.

✓ Answer key on Page 130

Section 135-b - Advertising by notaries public

1. The provisions of this section shall not apply to attorneys-at-law, admitted to practice in the state of New York.

2. A notary public who advertises his or her services as a notary public in a language other than English shall post with such advertisement a notice in such other language the following statement: "I am not an attorney licensed to practice law and may not give legal advice about immigration or any other legal matter or accept fees for legal advice."

3. A notary public shall not use terms in a foreign language in any advertisement for his or her services as a notary public that mean or imply that the notary public is an attorney licensed to practice in the state of New York or in any jurisdiction of the United States. The secretary shall designate by rule or regulation the terms in a foreign language that shall be deemed to mean or imply that a notary public is licensed to practice law in the state of New York and the use of which shall be prohibited by notary publics who are subject to this section.

4. For purposes of this section, "advertisement" shall mean and include material designed to give notice of or to promote or describe the services offered by a notary public for profit and shall include business cards, brochures, and notices, whether in print or electronic form.

5. Any person who violates any provision of this section or any rule or regulation promulgated by the secretary may be liable for civil penalty of up to one thousand dollars. The secretary of state may suspend a notary public upon a second violation of any of the provisions of this section and may remove from office a notary public upon a third violation of any of the provisions of this section, provided that the notary public shall have been served with a copy of the charges against him or her and been given an opportunity to be heard. The civil penalty provided for by this subdivision shall be recoverable in an action instituted by the attorney general on his or her own initiative or at the request of the secretary.

6. The secretary may promulgate rules and regulations governing the provisions of this section, including the size and type of statements that a notary public is required by this section to post.

SUMMARY

1. Attorneys-at-law admitted in New York are exempt from the restrictions in this section related to notary public advertising and practice.

2. Notaries public who advertise in languages other than English must include the following statement clarifying they are not attorneys and cannot provide legal advice or accept fees for such advice:

"I am not an attorney licensed to practice law and may not give legal advice about immigration or any other legal matter or accept fees for legal advice."

3. Notaries public must not imply in any non-English advertisements that they are licensed attorneys. The Secretary will specify which foreign language terms are prohibited for notaries to use.

4. "Advertisement" is defined broadly to include all promotional materials like business cards and brochures, in both print and electronic formats, that market a notary's for-profit services.

5. Violation of these regulations can result in a civil penalty up to $1,000. Repeated violations can lead to suspension or removal from the notary public office after due process.

6. The Secretary has the authority to issue further rules and regulations regarding advertising, including the required size and type of disclaimer statements by notaries.

TRUE OR FALSE?

15. A notary public who is also an attorney may not advertise legal services in a foreign language.

✓ Answer key on Page 130

Section 135-c – Electronic notarization

1. Definitions.
    a. "Communication technology" means an electronic device or process that: (i) allows a notary public and a remotely located individual to communicate with each other simultaneously by sight and sound; and (ii) when necessary and consistent with other applicable law, facilitates communication with a remotely located individual who has a vision, hearing, or speech impairment.
    b. "Electronic" shall have the same meaning as set forth in subdivision one of section three hundred two of the state technology law.
    c. "Electronic record" means information that is created, generated, sent, communicated, received or stored by electronic means.
    d. "Electronic notarial act" means an official act by a notary public, physically present in the state of New York, on or involving an electronic record and using means authorized by the secretary of state.
    e. "Electronic notary public" or "electronic notary" means a notary public who has registered with the secretary of state the capability of performing electronic notarial acts.
    f. "Electronic signature" shall have the same meaning as set forth in subdivision three of section three hundred two of the state technology law.
    g. "Principal" means an individual:
        i. whose signature is reflected on a record that is notarized;

ii. who has taken an oath or affirmation administered by a notary public; or
iii. whose signature is reflected on a record that is notarized after the individual has taken an oath or affirmation administered by a notary public.
h. "Record" means information that is inscribed on a tangible medium or that is stored in an electronic or other medium and is retrievable in perceivable form.

2. Any notary public qualified under this article is hereby authorized to perform an electronic notarial act by utilizing audio-video communication technology that allows the notary public to interact with a principal, provided that all conditions of this section are met.
   a. The methods for identifying document signers for an electronic notarization shall be the same as the methods required for a paper-based notarization; provided, however, an electronic notarial act conducted utilizing communication technology shall meet the standards which have been approved through regulation by the secretary of state as acceptable. Such regulations shall include, but not be limited to:
   i. that the signal transmission shall be secure from interception through lawful means by anyone other than the persons communicating;
   ii. that the communication technology shall permit the notary public to communicate with the principal live, in real time;
   iii. that the communication technology shall permit the notary to communicate with and identify the remotely located individual at the time of the notarial act; and
   iv. a standard that requires two or more different processes for authenticating the identity of a remotely located individual utilizing technology to detect and deter fraud, but which may allow a notary public's personal knowledge of a document signer to satisfy such requirement.
   b. If video and audio conference technology has been used to ascertain a document signer's identity, the electronic notary shall keep a copy of the recording of the video and audio conference and a notation of the type of any other identification used. The recording shall be maintained for a period of at least ten years from the date of transaction.

3. Registration requirements.
   a. Before performing any electronic notarial act or acts, a notary public shall register the capability to notarize electronically with the secretary of state on a form prescribed by the secretary of state and upon payment of a fee which shall be set by regulation.

   b. In registering the capability to perform electronic notarial acts, the notary public shall provide the following information to the secretary of state, notary processing unit:
   i. the applicant's name as currently commissioned and complete mailing address;
   ii. the expiration date of the notary public's commission and signature of the commissioned notary public;
   iii. the applicant's e-mail address;

iv. the description of the electronic technology or technologies to be used in attaching the notary public's electronic signature to the electronic record; and
v. an exemplar of the notary public's electronic signature, which shall contain the notary public's name and any necessary instructions or techniques that allow the notary public's electronic signature to be read.

4. Types of electronic notarial acts.
    a. Any notarial act authorized by section one hundred thirty-five of this article may be performed electronically as prescribed by this section if: (i) for execution of any instrument in writing, under applicable law that document may be signed with an electronic signature and the notary public is reasonably able to confirm that such instrument is the same instrument in which the principal made a statement or on which the principal executed a signature; and (ii) the electronic notary public is located within the state of New York at the time of the performance of an electronic notarial act using communication technology, regardless of the location of the document signer. If the principal is outside the United States, the record or subject of the notarial act:
    1. is to be filed with or relates to a matter before a public official or court, governmental entity, or other entity subject to the jurisdiction of the United States; or
    2. shall involve property located in the territorial jurisdiction of the United States or shall involve a transaction substantially connected with the United States.
    b. An electronic notarial act performed using communication technology pursuant to this section satisfies any requirement of law of this state that a document signer personally appear before, be in the presence of, or be in a single time and place with a notary public at the time of the performance of the notarial act.

5. Form and manner of performing the electronic notarial act.
    a. When performing an electronic notarial act relating to execution of instruments in writing, a notary public shall apply an electronic signature, which shall be attached to the electronic record such that removal or alteration of such electronic signature is detectable and will render evidence of alteration of the document containing the notary signature which may invalidate the electronic notarial act.

    b. The notary public's electronic signature is deemed to be reliable if the standards which have been approved through regulation by the secretary of state have been met. Such regulations shall include, but not be limited to, the requirements that such electronic signature be:
        i. unique to the notary public;
        ii. capable of independent verification
        iii. retained under the notary public's sole control
        iv. attached to the electronic record; and

      v. linked to the data in such a manner that any subsequent alterations to the underlying document are detectable and may invalidate the electronic notarial act.
  c. The notary public's electronic signature shall be used only for the purpose of performing electronic notarial acts.
  d. The remote online notarial certificate for an electronic notarial act shall state that the person making the acknowledgement or making the oath appeared through use of communication technology.
  e. The secretary shall adopt rules necessary to establish standards, procedures, practices, forms, and records relating to a notary public's electronic signature. The notary public's electronic signature shall conform to any standards adopted by the secretary.

6. Recording of an electronic record.
  a. If otherwise required by law as a condition for recording that a document be an original document, printed on paper or another tangible medium, or be in writing, the requirement is satisfied by paper copy of an electronic record that complies with the requirements of this section.
  b. If otherwise required by law as a condition for recording, that a document be signed, the requirement may be satisfied by an electronic signature.
  c. A requirement that a document or a signature associated with a document be notarized, acknowledged, verified, witnessed, or made under oath is satisfied if the electronic signature of the person authorized to perform that act, and all other information required to be included, is attached to or logically associated with the document or signature. A physical or electronic image of a stamp, impression, or seal need not accompany an electronic signature if the notary has attached an electronic notarial certificate that meets the requirements of this section.
  d.
      i. A notary public may certify that a tangible copy of the signature page and document type of an electronic record remotely notarized by such notary public is an accurate copy of such electronic record. Such certification must (1) be dated and signed by the notary public in the same manner as the official signature of the notary public provided to the secretary of state pursuant to section one hundred thirty-one of this article, and (2) comply with section one hundred thirty-seven of this article.
      ii. A county clerk, city registrar, or other recording officer where applicable shall accept for recording a tangible copy of an electronic record and that is otherwise eligible to be recorded under the laws of this state if the record has been certified by a notary public or other individual authorized to perform a notarial act.
      iii. A certification in substantially the following form is sufficient for the purposes of this subdivision:

CERTIFICATE OF AUTHENTICITY
State of New York   )

) ss.:
County of   )

On this .... day of .... in the year ...., I certify that the signature page of the attached record (entitled ....) (dated ....) is a true and correct copy of the signatures affixed to an electronic record printed by me or under my supervision. I further certify that, at the time of printing, no security features present on the electronic record indicated any changes or errors in an electronic signature in the electronic record after its creation or execution.
(Signature and title of notary public)
(official stamp or registration number, with the expiration date of the notary public's commission)

7. Change of e-mail address. Within five days after the change of an electronic notary public's e-mail address, the notary public shall electronically transmit to the secretary of state a notice of the change, signed with the notary public's official electronic signature.

8. No notary public or business employing the services of a notary public operating in the state of New York shall exclusively require notarial transactions to utilize electronic notarization.

9. Nothing in this section shall be construed as requiring any notary public to perform a notarial act using electronic communication technology. A notary public may refuse to perform such a notarial act if the notary public is not satisfied that (a) the principal is competent or has the capacity to execute a record, or (b) the principal's signature is knowingly and voluntarily made.

10. Notwithstanding article nine of the real property law or any other law to the contrary, any act performed in conformity with this section shall satisfy any requirements at law that a principal personally appear before, be in the presence of, or be in a single time and place with a notary public at the time of the performance of the notarial act, unless a law expressly excludes the authorization provided for in this section.

SUMMARY

1. Definitions.
   a. **Communication Technology**: An electronic method enabling notaries and individuals to interact via sight and sound, also accommodating those with vision, hearing, or speech impairments.
   b. **Electronic**: Of or relating to technology having electrical, digital, magnetic, wireless, optical, electromagnetic, or similar capabilities.

c. **Electronic Record**: Information created or stored by digital means.
d. **Electronic Notarial Act**: A notary act involving an electronic record, performed within New York State.
e. **Electronic Notary Public**: A notary registered to perform notarial acts on electronic records.
f. **Electronic Signature**: An electronic sound, symbol, or process, attached to or logically associated with an electronic record and executed or adopted by a person with the intent to sign the record.
g. **Principal**: An individual involved with a notarized record or who has taken an oath via a notary.
h. **Record**: Information that is tangible or stored electronically and retrievable.

2. **Electronic Notarial Act Authorization**: Notaries can perform electronic notarial acts using audio-video technology if they adhere to prescribed conditions, including secure communication and identity verification standards.
    a. **Identification Methods**: Identifying people who sign documents electronically should be done the same way as with paper documents. However, when using video technology, notaries must use secure communication, talk to the person live, confirm the person's identity in real-time, and use at least two ways to check identity to prevent fraud. Knowing the person may count as one method of identification.
    b. **Record-Keeping**: When a notary uses video calls to identify someone, they must save the video and audio of the call and any other ID methods used. This record has to be kept for at least ten years.

3. **Registration Requirements.**
    a. Notaries who want to notarize documents electronically need to officially register this service with the state's secretary and pay a fee.
    b. Required registration information includes the notary's name, address, commission expiration date, email, description of technology used, and an example of the electronic signature.

4. **Types of Electronic Notarial Acts.**
    a. Notaries can perform their duties online for any written document that the law allows to be signed electronically, as long as the notary can be sure it's the same document the person intended to sign. The notary must be in New York when doing this, but the person signing can be anywhere. If the person signing is outside the U.S., the document must either be related to something under U.S. jurisdiction or involve U.S. property or transactions.
    b. When a notary uses online video and audio to perform their duties, it meets the legal requirement that normally the person signing needs to be in the same place as the notary.

5. **Form and Manner of Electronic Notarial Acts.**
   a. Notaries must apply an electronic signature to notarize documents electronically.
   b. The electronic signature must be reliable, unique, verifiable, and solely under the notary's control.
   c. The electronic signature should only be used for notarial acts.
   d. Certificates must indicate the use of communication technology.
   e. Standards and procedures for electronic signatures are set by the secretary.

6. **Recording of Electronic Records.**
   a. If the law requires an original, written document for recording, you can use a paper printout of the electronic record as long as it follows the rules of this section.
   b. If a signed document is needed for recording, you can use an electronic signature instead.
   c. If a document needs to be notarized or verified, it's okay if the person doing it uses an electronic signature and includes all the needed details with the document. You don't need a physical stamp or seal if there's an electronic certificate from the notary.
   d. Notaries can confirm that a paper printout is a true copy of an electronic record. This confirmation has to be signed and dated just like the notary's official signature filed with the state. Clerks and other officials should accept these certified printouts for recording. They need to use a specific statement of authenticity that confirms the signatures are correct and the electronic record hasn't been tampered with after it was signed.

7. **Change of Email Address**: Notaries must update their email address with the secretary of state within five days of change, using their official electronic signature.

8. **No Exclusive Electronic Notarization Requirement**: Notaries or their employers cannot mandate electronic notarization exclusively in New York State.

9. **Voluntary Electronic Notarization**: Notaries are not compelled to perform electronic notarizations and may refuse based on concerns over the principal's competence or voluntariness.

10. **Legal Conformance**: Acts performed in compliance with this section satisfy the requirement of the principal's physical presence before a notary, unless explicitly excluded by law.

TRUE OR FALSE?

16. A notary public can refuse to perform an electronic notarial act if they are not satisfied with the principal's capacity or willingness to sign.

✓ Answer key on Page 130

Section 136 - Notarial fees

A notary public shall be entitled to the following fees:

1. For administering an oath or affirmation, and certifying the same when required, except where another fee is specifically prescribed by statute, $2.

2. For taking and certifying the acknowledgment or proof of execution of a written instrument, by one person, $2, and by each additional person, $2, for swearing such witness thereto, $2.

3. For electronic notarial services, established in section one hundred thirty-five-c of this chapter, a fee set through regulation by the secretary of state.

SUMMARY

A notary public is entitled to the following fees:

1. For administering an oath or affirmation, and certifying the same, except when another fee is prescribed by statute, $2.

2. For taking and certifying the acknowledgment or proof of execution of a written instrument, for one person, $2, and each additional person, $2, and for swearing a witness, $2.

3. For providing electronic notarial services as specified in section 135-c, the Secretary of State will determine and set the applicable fees through regulation.

TRUE OR FALSE?

17. A notary public may charge $2 for administering an oath.

✓ Answer key on Page 130

Section 137 - Statement as to authority of notaries public

In exercising powers pursuant to this article, a notary public, in addition to the venue of the act and signature of such notary public, shall print, typewrite, stamp, or affix by electronic means where performing an electronic notarial act in conformity with section one hundred thirty-five-c of the executive law, beneath their signature in black ink, the notary public's name, the words "Notary Public State of New York," the name of the county in which such notary public originally qualified, and the expiration date of such notary public's commission and, in addition, wherever required, a notary public shall also include the name of any county in which such notary public's certificate of official character is filed, using the words "Certificate filed ……………… County."

A notary public who is duly licensed as an attorney and counselor at law in this State may, substitute the words "Attorney and Counselor at Law" for the words "Notary Public."

A notary public who has qualified or who has filed a certificate of official character in the office of the clerk in a county or counties within the City of New York must also affix to each instrument such notary public's official number or numbers in black ink, as assigned by the clerk or clerks of such county or counties at the time such notary qualified in such county or counties and, if the instrument is to be recorded in an office of the register of the City of New York in any county within such city and the notary has been given a number or numbers by such register or his predecessors in any county or counties, when the notary public's autographed signature and certificate are filed in such office or offices pursuant to this chapter, the notary public shall also affix such number or numbers. No official act of such notary public shall be held invalid on account of the failure to comply with these provisions. If any notary public shall willfully fail to comply with any of the provisions of this section, the notary public shall be subject to disciplinary action by the secretary of state.

In all the courts within this State the certificate of a notary public, over the signature of the notary public, shall be received as presumptive evidence of the facts contained in such certificate; provided, that any person interested as a party to a suit may contradict, by other evidence, the certificate of a notary public.

SUMMARY

In performing duties, a notary public, in addition to the location of their act and signature, shall print, typewrite, or stamp beneath their signature in black ink, his name, the words **"Notary Public State of New York**," the name of the county which he first qualified, date commission expires, and where required, the name of any county where their certificate of official character is filed using the words **"Certificate filed…County."** This is also called the statement of authority.

An attorney in the state may substitute notary public for the words **"Attorney and Counselor at Law."**

A notary public who has qualified or filed a certificate in a county within New York City must also affix their official number in black ink, given by the clerks in the county at the time the notary qualified.

No official act will be deemed invalid for failure to comply with this section.

Any notary public who willfully fails to comply with this section shall be subject to discipline by the Secretary of State.

In all courts in the state, the certificate of a notary public over his signature shall be received as presumptive evidence of the facts within, provided that another party may contradict with other evidence the certificate of a notary public.

TRUE OR FALSE?

18. "Notary Public State of New York" must be included on every signature, regardless if the notary is also an attorney.

✓ Answer key on Page 130

Section 138 - Powers of notaries public or other officers who are stockholders, directors, officers or employees of a corporation

A notary public, justice of the supreme court, a judge, clerk, deputy clerk, or special deputy clerk of a court, an official examiner of title, or the mayor or recorder of a city, a justice of the peace, surrogate, special surrogate, special county judge, or commissioner of deeds, who is a stockholder, director, officer or employee of a corporation may take the acknowledgment or proof of any party to a written instrument executed to or by such corporation, or administer an oath of any other stockholder, director, officer, employee or agent of such corporation, and such notary public may protest for non- acceptance or non-payment, bills of exchange, drafts, checks, notes and other negotiable instruments owned or held for collection by such corporation; but none of the officers above named shall take the acknowledgment or proof of a written instrument by or to a corporation of which he is a stockholder, director, officer or employee, if such officer taking such acknowledgment or proof be a party executing such instrument, either individually or as representative of such corporation, nor shall a notary public protest any negotiable instruments owned or held for collection by such corporation, if such notary public be individually a party to such instrument, or have a financial interest in the subject of same.

All such acknowledgments or proofs of deeds, mortgages or other written instruments, relating to real property heretofore taken before any of the officers aforesaid are confirmed. This act shall not affect any action or legal proceeding now pending.

SUMMARY

A notary public, justice of the supreme court, judge, clerk, deputy clerk, special deputy clerk of court, official examiner of title, the mayor or recorder of a city, justice of the peace, surrogate, special surrogate, special county judge, or commissioner of deeds, who is a stockholder, director, officer or employee of a corporation may take the acknowledgment of any party to a written instrument executed by such corporation or administer the oath of any shareholder, director, officer, employee, or agent of such corporation.

A notary public may protest for non-payment, but no officer shall take the acknowledgment of a corporation in which he is involved.

TRUE OR FALSE?

19. A notary public who is a stockholder of a company may take proof to a written instrument executed to that company.

✓ Answer key on Page 130

Section 142-a - Validity of acts of notaries public and commissioners of deeds notwithstanding certain defects

1. Except as provided in subdivision three of this section, the official certificates and other acts heretofore or hereafter made or performed of notaries public and commissioners of deeds heretofore or hereafter and prior to the time of their acts appointed or commissioned as such shall not be deemed invalid, impaired or in any manner defective, so far as they may be affected, impaired or questioned by reason of defects described in subdivision two of this section.

2. This section shall apply to the following defects:

   a. ineligibility of the notary public or commissioner of deeds to be appointed or commissioned as such;
   b. misnomer or misspelling of name or other error made in his appointment or commission;
   c. omission of the notary public or commissioner of deeds to take or file his official oath or otherwise qualify;

    d. expiration of his term, commission or appointment;
    e. vacating of his office by change of his residence, by acceptance of another public office, or by other action on his part;
    f. the fact that the action was taken outside the jurisdiction where the notary public or commissioner of deeds was authorized to act.

3. No person shall be entitled to assert the effect of this section to overcome a defect described in subdivision two if he knew of the defect or if the defect was apparent on the face of the certificate of the notary public or commissioner of deeds; provided however, that this subdivision shall not apply after the expiration of six months from the date of the act of the notary public or commissioner of deeds.

4. After the expiration of six months from the date of the official certificate or other act of the commissioner of deeds, subdivision one of this section shall be applicable to a defect consisting in omission of the certificate of a commissioner of deeds to state the date on which and the place in which an act was done, or consisting of an error in such statement.

5. This section does not relieve any notary public or commissioner of deeds from criminal liability imposed by reason of his act, or enlarge the actual authority of any such officer, nor limit any other statute or rule of law by reason of which the act of a notary public or commissioner of deeds, or the record thereof, is valid or is deemed valid in any case.

SUMMARY

1. Except as provided in subdivision 3, the official certificate and other acts made by notaries and commissioners of deeds shall not be invalid, impaired, or questioned because of defects unless they satisfy a requirement of subdivision 2.

2. This section lists applicable defects:

    a. Ineligibility of the notary or commissioner of deeds to be appointed as such;
    b. Misnomer or misspelling of the name or other error made;
    c. Omission of the notary or commissioner to take or file his oath;
    d. Expiration of his term, commission, or appointment;
    e. Vacating the post by moving or accepting a new position;
    f. The action was outside the jurisdiction of the notary public or commissioner.

3. Nobody can claim relief due to defect if they knew of the defect or it was apparent on the certificate; provided that this subdivision shall not apply 6 months after the act.

4. After 6 months from the act, subdivision 1 shall apply to a defect of omission of the certificate of a commissioner of deeds to state the date and place the act was done, or consisting of an error in such statement.

5. This does not relieve a notary public or commission from criminal liability based on his act, enlarge authority, or limit any other statute or law that makes his actions valid or invalid.

TRUE OR FALSE?

20.   A person can file a claim for defect if the defect was known about upon when it occurred.

✓ Answer key on Page 130

REAL PROPERTY LAW

Section 290 - Definitions; effect of article

3. The term "conveyance" includes every written instrument, by which any estate or interest in real property is created, transferred, mortgaged or assigned, or by which the title to any real property may be affected, including an instrument in execution of power, although the power be one of revocation only, and an instrument postponing or subordinating a mortgage lien; except a will, a lease for a term not exceeding three years, an executory contract for the sale or purchase of lands, and an instrument containing a power to convey real property as the agent or attorney for the owner of such property.

SUMMARY

3. The term "conveyance" refers to any written document that creates, changes, transfers, mortgages, or assigns an interest in real property, or affects the title to real property. This includes documents executing power, even if it is only for revocation, and documents that change the priority of mortgage liens. However, it does not include wills, leases not exceeding three years, contracts for the sale or purchase of land not yet completed, or documents that grant the authority to transfer real property on behalf of the owner.

TRUE OR FALSE?

21. A lease for 2 years is an example of a conveyance.

✓ Answer key on Page 130

Section 298 - Acknowledgments and proofs within the state

The acknowledgment or proof, within this state, of a conveyance of real property situate in this State may be made:

1. At any place within the state, before
    a. a justice of the supreme court;
    b. an official examiner of title;
    c. an official referee; or
    d. a notary public.

2. Within the district wherein such officer is authorized to perform official duties, before
    a. a judge or clerk of any court of record;

b. a commissioner of deeds outside of the City of New York, or a commissioner of deeds of the City of New York within the five counties comprising the City of New York;
c. the mayor or recorder of a city;
d. a surrogate, special surrogate, or special county judge; or
e. the county clerk or other recording officer of a county.

3. Before a justice of the peace, town councilman, village police justice or a judge of any court of inferior local jurisdiction, anywhere within the county containing the town, village or city in which he is authorized to perform official duties.

SUMMARY

The acknowledgment or verification of documents related to the conveyance of real property located in New York State can be made anywhere within the state before a justice of the supreme court, an official examiner of title, an official referee, or a notary public. Additionally, within the jurisdiction where the officer has official authority, it can be done before a judge or clerk of any court of record, a commissioner of deeds (outside of New York City or within it, respecting the five boroughs), the mayor or recorder of a city, a surrogate or county judge, or the county clerk. Finally, a justice of the peace, town councilman, village police justice, or a judge of a local court of inferior jurisdiction can also perform such acknowledgment within the county of their official duties.

TRUE OR FALSE?

22. A notary public may certify the acknowledgment of proof for any conveyance within the state.

✓ Answer key on Page 130

Section 302 - Acknowledgments and proofs by married women

The acknowledgment or proof of a conveyance of real property, within the state, or of any other written instrument, may be made by a married woman the same as if unmarried.

SUMMARY

The acknowledgment of proof of conveyance made by married women, same as if unmarried.

TRUE OR FALSE?

23. Married women have the same rights as unmarried in conveyances.

✓ Answer key on Page 130

Section 303 - Requisites of acknowledgments

An acknowledgment must not be taken by any officer unless he knows or has satisfactory evidence, that the person making it is the person described in and who executed such instrument.

SUMMARY

An acknowledgment must not be taken by anyone unless they know or have evidence the person making it is the person described.

TRUE OR FALSE?

24. A notary public does not need to verify the identity of the person they are taking an acknowledgment from.

✓ Answer key on Page 130

Section 304 - Proof by subscribing witness

When the execution of a conveyance is proved by a subscribing witness, such witness must state his own place of residence, and if his place of residence is in a city, the street and street number, if any thereof, and that he knew the person described in and who executed the conveyance. The proof must not be taken unless the officer is personally acquainted with such witness, or has satisfactory evidence that he is the same person, who was a subscribing witness to the conveyance.

SUMMARY

When there is a subscribing witness in the execution of a conveyance, the witness must state his full address, and that he knows the person who executed the conveyance.

The officer must know or have proof that he is the same person who is listed as a subscribing witness.

TRUE OR FALSE?

25. A subscribing witness must know the person executing the conveyance.

✓ Answer key on Page 130

Section 306 - Certificate of acknowledgment or proof

A person taking the acknowledgment or proof of a conveyance must endorse thereupon or attach thereto, a certificate, signed by himself, stating all the matters required to be done, known, or proved on the taking of such acknowledgment or proof; together with the name and substance of the testimony of each witness examined before him, and if a subscribing witness, his place of residence.

SUMMARY

A person taking the acknowledgment or proof of conveyance must include a signed certificate stating the details of the conveyance with the name and testimony of the witnesses and the addresses of any witnesses who signed.

TRUE OR FALSE?

26. When taking the acknowledgment or proof of conveyance, a notary public needs to include a certificate with the details of the conveyance, and the name and testimony of the witnesses only.

✓ Answer key on Page 130

Section 309-a - Uniform forms of certificates of acknowledgment or proof within this state

1. The certificate of an acknowledgment, within this State, or a conveyance or other instrument in respect to real property situate in this State, by a person, must conform substantially with the following form, the blanks being properly filled:

State of New York)
) ss.:
County of ....)
    On the ...... day of ...... in the year ...... before me, the undersigned, personally appeared ......, personally known to me or proved to me on the basis of satisfactory

evidence to be the individual(s) whose name(s) is (are) subscribed to the within instrument and acknowledged to me that he/she/they executed the same in his/her/their capacity(ies), and that by his/her/their signature(s) on the instrument, the individual(s), or the person upon behalf of which the individual(s) acted, executed the instrument.

(Signature and office of individual taking acknowledgment.)

2. The certificate for a proof of execution by a subscribing witness, within this state, of a conveyance or other instrument made by any person in respect to real property situate in this state, must conform substantially with the following form, the blanks being properly filled:

State of New York)
) ss.:
County of . . . .)

On the . . . . . . day of . . . . . . in the year . . . . . . before me, the undersigned, personally appeared . . . . . ., the subscribing witness to the foregoing instrument, with whom I am personally acquainted, who, being by me duly sworn, did depose and say that he/she/they reside(s) in . . . . . . (if the place of residence is in a city, include the street and street number, if any, thereof); that he/she/they know(s) . . . . . . to be the individual described in and who executed the foregoing instrument; that said subscribing witness was present and saw said . . . . . . execute the same; and that said witness at the same time subscribed his/her/their name(s) as a witness thereto.

(Signature and office of individual taking proof).

3. A certificate of an acknowledgment or proof taken under Section 300 of this article shall include the additional information required by that section.

4. For the purposes of this section, the term "person" means any corporation, joint stock company, estate, general partnership (including any registered limited liability partnership or foreign limited liability partnership), limited liability company (including a professional service limited liability company), foreign limited liability company (including a foreign professional service limited liability company), joint venture, limited partnership, natural person, attorney in fact, real estate investment trust, business trust or other trust, custodian, nominee or any other individual or entity in its own or any representative capacity.

SUMMARY

1. The certificate of an acknowledgment in NYS or a conveyance must substantially conform the following form (blank spaces filled appropriately):

State of New York)
) ss.:
County of . . . .)

On the ...... day of ...... in the year ...... before me, the undersigned, personally appeared ......, personally known to me or proved to me on the basis of satisfactory evidence to be the individual(s) whose name(s) is (are) subscribed to the within instrument and acknowledged to me that he/she/they executed the same in his/her/their capacity(ies), and that by his/her/their signature(s) on the instrument, the individual(s), or the person upon behalf of which the individual(s) acted, executed the instrument.
(Signature and office of individual taking acknowledgment.)

2. The certificate for proof of execution by a subscribing witness for a conveyance in respect to real property must conform the following form (blank spaces filled appropriately):

State of New York)
) ss.:
County of ....)
On the ...... day of ...... in the year ...... before me, the undersigned, personally appeared ......, the subscribing witness to the foregoing instrument, with whom I am personally acquainted, who, being by me duly sworn, did depose and say that he/she/they reside(s) in ...... (if the place of residence is in a city, include the street and street number, if any, thereof); that he/she/they know(s) ...... to be the individual described in and who executed the foregoing instrument; that said subscribing witness was present and saw said ...... execute the same; and that said witness at the same time subscribed his/her/their name(s) as a witness thereto.
(Signature and office of individual taking proof).

3. A certificate of acknowledgment taken under section 300 shall include the required information.

4. For this section, the term "person" means any individual or entity in its own or any representative capacity.

TRUE OR FALSE?

27. If following the format in 309-a, a notary public does not need to include any other information.

✓ Answer key on Page 130

Section 309-b - Uniform forms of certificates of acknowledgment or proof without this state

1. The certificate of an acknowledgment, without this State, of a conveyance or other instrument with respect to real property situate in this State, by a person, may conform substantially with the following form, the blanks being properly filled:

State, District of Columbia,)
Territory, Possession, or   ) ss.:
Foreign Country   )

On the ...... day of ...... in the year ...... before me, the undersigned, personally appeared ......, personally known to me or proved to me on the basis of satisfactory evidence to be the individual(s) whose name(s) is (are) subscribed to the within instrument and acknowledged to me that he/she/they executed the same in his/her/their capacity(ies), and that by his/her/their signature(s) on the instrument, the individual(s), or the person upon behalf of which the individual(s) acted, executed the instrument.

(Signature and office of individual taking acknowledgment.)

2. The certificate for a proof of execution by a subscribing witness, without this State, of a conveyance or other instrument made by any person in respect to real property situate in this State, may conform substantially with the following form, the blanks being properly filled:

State, District of Columbia,)
Territory, Possession, or   ) ss.:
Foreign Country   )

On the ...... day of ...... in the year ...... before me, the undersigned, personally appeared ......, the subscribing witness to the foregoing instrument, with whom I am personally acquainted, who, being by me duly sworn, did depose and say that he/she resides in ...... (if the place of residence is in a city, include the street and street number, if any, thereof); that he/she knows ...... to be the individual described in and who executed the foregoing instrument; that said subscribing witness was present and saw said ...... execute the same; and that said witness at the same time subscribed his/her name as a witness thereto.

(Signature and office of individual taking proof.)

3. No provision of this section shall be construed to:

  a. modify the choice of laws afforded by Section 299-a and 301-a of this article pursuant to which an acknowledgment or proof may be taken;

  b. modify any requirement of Section 307 of this article;

  c. modify any requirement for a seal imposed by subdivision one of Section 308 of this article;

d. modify any requirement concerning a certificate of authentication imposed by Section 308, 311, 312, 314, or 318 of this article; or

e. modify any requirement imposed by any provision of this article when the certificate of acknowledgment or proof purports to be taken in the manner prescribed by the laws of another state, the District of Columbia, territory, possession, or foreign country.

4. A certificate of an acknowledgment or proof taken under Section 300 of this article shall include the additional information required by that section.

5. For the purposes of this section, the term "person" means a person as defined in subdivision 4 of Section 309-a of this article.

6. The inclusion within the body (other than the jurat) of a certificate of acknowledgment or proof made under this section or the city or other political subdivision and the state or country or other place the acknowledgment was taken shall be deemed. A non-substantial variance from the form of a certificate authorized by this section.

SUMMARY

1. The certificate of an acknowledgment, without this state, for a conveyance may substantially conform this form (blank spaces filled appropriately):

State, District of Columbia,)
Territory, Possession, or   ) ss.:
Foreign Country   )
On the ...... day of ...... in the year ...... before me, the undersigned, personally appeared ......, personally known to me or proved to me on the basis of satisfactory evidence to be the individual(s) whose name(s) is (are) subscribed to the within instrument and acknowledged to me that he/she/they executed the same in his/her/their capacity(ies), and that by his/her/their signature(s) on the instrument, the individual(s), or the person upon behalf of which the individual(s) acted, executed the instrument.
(Signature and office of individual taking acknowledgment.)

2. The certificate for a proof of execution by a subscribing witness, without the state, should conform to the following form (blank spaces filled appropriately):

State, District of Columbia,)
Territory, Possession, or   ) ss.:
Foreign Country   )
On the ...... day of ...... in the year ...... before me, the undersigned, personally appeared ......, the subscribing witness to the foregoing instrument, with whom I am

personally acquainted, who, being by me duly sworn, did depose and say that he/she resides in . . . . . . (if the place of residence is in a city, include the street and street number, if any, thereof); that he/she knows . . . . . . to be the individual described in and who executed the foregoing instrument; that said subscribing witness was present and saw said . . . . . . execute the same; and that said witness at the same time subscribed his/her name as a witness thereto.

(Signature and office of individual taking proof.)

3. No provision of this section should be interpreted to:

   a. Modify the choice of law based on sections 299-a and 301-a of this article;
   b. Modify a requirement of section 307;
   c. Modify seal requirements of section 308;
   d. Modify certificate of authentication requirements of sections 308, 311, 312, 314, or 318;
   e. Modify any requirements of this article when following the law of another jurisdiction.

4. A certificate of acknowledgment or proof taken under section 300 shall include the additional information required.

5. For this section, a person is defined in subdivision 4 of section 309-a.

6. The inclusion of location within a proof of acknowledgment will be viewed as a non-substantial variance from the previous form.

TRUE OR FALSE?

28. Including the location of the proof of acknowledgment is a substantial error and variation from the template.

✓ Answer key on Page 130

Section 330 - Officers guilty of malfeasance liable for damages

An officer authorized to take the acknowledgment or proof of a conveyance or other instrument, or to certify such proof or acknowledgment, or to record the same, who is guilty of malfeasance or fraudulent practice in the execution of any duty prescribed by law in relation thereto, is liable in damages to the person injured.

SUMMARY

An officer authorized to take and acknowledgment of proof who is guilty of malfeasance or fraud is liable in damages to those injured.

TRUE OR FALSE?

29. A notary public guilty of fraud is liable for damages to the injured party.

✓ Answer key on Page 130

Section 333 - When conveyances of real property not to be recorded

2. A recording officer shall not record or accept for record any conveyance of real property, unless said conveyance in its entirety and the certificate of acknowledgment or proof and the authentication thereof, other than proper names therein which may be in another language provided they are written in English letters or characters, shall be in the English language, or unless such conveyance, certificate of acknowledgment or proof, and the authentication thereof be accompanied by and have attached thereto a translation in the English language duly executed and acknowledged by the person or persons making such conveyance and proved and authenticated, if need be, in the manner required of conveyances for recording in this state, or, unless such conveyance, certificate of acknowledgment or proof, and the authentication thereof be accompanied by and have attached thereto a translation in the English language made by a person duly designated for such purpose by the county judge of the county where it is desired to record such conveyance or a justice of the supreme court and be duly signed, acknowledged and certified under oath or upon affirmation by such person before such judge, to be a true and accurate translation and contain a certification of the designation of such person by such judge.

SUMMARY

2. A recording officer should not accept any conveyance of real property that is in a foreign language, other than names (provided they are written in English), unless an authenticated translation is given, or a translation is provided by a person duly appointed by the county judge of the county or justice of the supreme court and certified under oath to be a true and accurate translation.

TRUE OR FALSE?

30. A recording officer fluent in another language may accept a conveyance in that language.

✓ Answer key on Page 130

SPECIAL NOTE

By reason of changes in certain provisions of the Real Property Law, any and all limitations on the authority of a notary public to act as such in any part of the State have been removed; a notary public may now, in addition to administering oaths or taking affidavits anywhere in the State, take acknowledgments and proofs of conveyances anywhere in the State.

The need for a certificate of authentication of a county clerk as a prerequisite to recording or use in evidence in this State of the instrument acknowledged or proved has been abolished. The certificate of authentication may possibly be required where the instrument is to be recorded or used in evidence outside the jurisdiction of the State.

Effective September 23, 2012, recording officers (County Clerks) may receive and record digitized paper documents and electronic records affecting real property, including real property transfer documents such as deeds, mortgages, notes and accompanying documents. The Office of Information Technology Services (ITS) has promulgated rules and regulations to support the implementation of electronic recording by local recording officers.

Section 335 - Banking Law

If the rental fee of any safe deposit box is not paid, or after the termination of the lease for such box, and at least 30 days after giving proper notice to the lessee, the lessor (bank) may, in the presence of a notary public, open the safe deposit box, remove and inventory the contents. The notary public shall then file with the lessor a certificate under seal which states the date of the opening of the safe deposit box, the name of the lessee, and a list of the contents. Within 10 days of the opening of the safe deposit box, a copy of this certificate must be mailed to the lessee at his last known postal address.

SUMMARY

If the rental fee for a security box is not paid or after the termination of said rental and 30 days after giving notice, the bank may, with a notary public present, open the box, and remove and inventory contents.

The notary public shall then file with the bank, under seal, the name of the lessee and a list of contents which must be mailed to the lessee within 10 days.

TRUE OR FALSE?

31. A letter must be sent to the lessee of a security box within 30 days of the bank opening it.

✓ Answer key on Page 130

Rule 3113 - Civil Practice Law and Rules

This rule authorizes a deposition to be taken before a notary public in a civil proceeding.

SUMMARY

A notary public may take a deposition in a civil proceeding.

TRUE OR FALSE?

32. A notary public may take a deposition is a civil proceeding.

✓ Answer key on Page 130

Section 11 - Domestic Relations Law

A notary public has no authority to solemnize marriages; nor may a notary public take the acknowledgment of parties and witnesses to a written contract of marriage.

SUMMARY

A notary public has no authority to officiate marriages or take the acknowledgment of witnesses to a marriage contract.

TRUE OR FALSE?

33. A notary public may take the acknowledgment for witnesses of a marriage.

✓ Answer key on Page 130

Section 10 - Public Officers Law

Official oaths, permits the oath of a public officer to be administered by a notary public.

SUMMARY

The oath of a public officer can be administered by a notary public.

TRUE OR FALSE?

34. A notary public can administer the oath of a public officer.

✓ Answer key on Page 130

RESTRICTIONS AND VIOLATIONS

Restrictions and Violations		
Judiciary Law	484	None but Attorneys to Practice
Judiciary Law	485	Misdemeanor Violations
Judiciary Law	750	Powers of Courts to Punish
Public Officers Law	15	Notary Must Not Act Before Taking/Filing Oath
Public Officers Law	67	Fees of Public Officers
Public Officers Law	69	Fees Prohibited for Administering Certain Oaths
Penal Law	70.00	Sentence of Imprisonment for Felony
Penal Law	70.15	Sentences of Imprisonment for Misdemeanors
Penal Law	170.10	Forgery in the Second Degree
Penal Law	175.40	Issuing a False Certificate
Penal Law	195.00	Official Misconduct

JUDICIARY LAW

Section 484 - None but attorneys to practice in the state

No natural person shall ask or receive, directly or indirectly, compensation for appearing for a person other than himself as attorney in any court or before any magistrate, or for preparing deeds, mortgages, assignments, discharges, leases or any other instruments affecting real estate, wills, codicils, or any other instrument affecting the disposition of property after death, or decedents' estates, or pleadings of any kind in any action brought before any court of record in this state, or make it a business to practice for another as an attorney in any court or before any magistrate unless he has been regularly admitted to practice, as an attorney or counselor, in the courts of record in the state; but nothing in this section shall apply

    1. to officers of societies for the prevention of cruelty, duly appointed, when exercising the special powers conferred upon such corporations under Section 1403 of the Not-for-Profit Corporation Law; or

    2. to law students who have completed at least 2 semesters of law school or persons who have graduated from a law school, who have taken the examination for admittance to practice law in the courts of record in the state immediately available after graduation from law school, or the examination immediately available after being notified by the board of law examiners that they failed to pass said exam, and who have not been notified by the board of law examiners that they have failed to pass two such examinations, acting under the supervision of a legal aid organization, when such students and persons are acting under a program approved by the appellate division of the supreme court of the department in which the principal office of such organization is located and specifying the extent to which such students and persons may engage in activities prohibited by this statute; or

    3. to persons who have graduated from a law school approved pursuant to the rules of the court of appeals for the admission of attorneys and counselors-at-law and who have taken the examination for admission to practice as an attorney and counselor-at-law immediately available after graduation from law school or the examination immediately available after being notified by the board of law examiners that they failed to pass said exam, and who have not been notified by the board of law examiners that they have failed to pass two such examinations, when such persons are acting under the supervision of the state or a subdivision thereof or of any officer or agency of the state or a subdivision thereof, pursuant to a program approved by the appellate division of the supreme court of the department within which such activities are taking place and specifying the extent to which they may engage in activities otherwise prohibited by this statute and those powers of the supervising governmental entity or officer in connection with which they may engage in such activities.

SUMMARY

No person should receive compensation for appearing for another person as an attorney in court, or for preparing real estate transactions, or any matter brought before a court, unless he is an attorney admitted to practice in NYS. This does not apply to:

1. Officers of society for the prevention of cruelty appointed when exercising special powers under section 1403 of the Not-for-Profit Corporation Law, or

2. Law students who have completed 2 semesters or have graduated from law school and took the bar after graduation but failed (only once) and are working under the supervision of a legal aid organization when the program has been approved by the appellate division of the supreme court; or

3. A graduate of law school who took the bar after graduation but failed (only once) and is working under the supervision of the state when it was approved by the appellate division of the supreme court.

TRUE OR FALSE?

35. A law student may work under the supervision of an appellate court-approved legal aid organization after 1 semester of school.

✓ Answer key on Page 130

Section 485 - Violation of certain preceding sections a misdemeanor

Any person violating the provisions of Section 478, 479, 480, 481, 482, 483 or 484, shall be guilty of a misdemeanor.

SUMMARY

Anyone violating the provisions of sections 478, 479, 480, 481, 482, 483 or 484 shall be guilty of a misdemeanor.

TRUE OR FALSE?

36. Violation of section 484 is a felony.

✓ Answer key on Page 130

Section 750 - Power of courts to punish for criminal contempts

The supreme court has power under this section to punish for a criminal contempt any person who unlawfully practices or assumes to practice law; and a proceeding under this subdivision may be instituted on the court's own motion or on the motion of any officer charged with the duty of investigating or prosecuting unlawful practice of law, or by any bar association incorporated under the laws of this State.

SUMMARY

The supreme court has the power to punish for criminal contempt anyone who practices law unlawfully, and a proceeding may be initiated by the court's own motion, or anyone charged to investigate the unlawful practice of law in NYS.

TRUE OR FALSE?

37. The supreme court may punish individuals for unlawful practice of law.

✓ Answer key on Page 130

Illegal practice of law by notary public

To make it a business to practice as an attorney at law, not being a lawyer, is a crime. "Counsel and advice, the drawing of agreements, the organization of corporations and preparing papers connected therewith, the drafting of legal documents of all kinds, including wills, are activities which have been long classed as law practice." (*People v. Alfani*, 227 NY 334, 339.)

SUMMARY

It is a crime to practice law as an attorney while not being a lawyer.

TRUE OR FALSE?

38. A notary public who is not a lawyer may draft legal documents for a friend's business.

✓ Answer key on Page 130

Wills

The execution of wills under the supervision of a notary public acting in effect as a lawyer, "cannot be too strongly condemned, not only for the reason that it means an invasion of the legal profession, but for the fact that testators thereby run the risk of frustrating their own solemnly declared intentions and rendering worthless maturely considered plans for the disposition of estates whose creation may have been the fruit of lives of industry and self-denial." (*Matter of Flynn*, 142 Misc. 7.)

PUBLIC OFFICERS LAWS

Notary must not act before taking and filing oath of office. The Public Officers Law (Section 15) provides that a person who executes any of the functions of a public office without having taken and duly filed the required oath of office, as prescribed by law, is guilty of a misdemeanor. A notary public is a public officer.

SUMMARY

A notary public is guilty of a misdemeanor if he performs any duties of a notary before taking and filing oath of office.

TRUE OR FALSE?

39. A notary public may administer an oath the same day his oath of office has been taken and filed.

✓ Answer key on Page 130

Section 67 - Fees of public officers

1. Each public officer upon whom a duty is expressly imposed by law, must execute the same without fee or reward, except where a fee or other compensation therefor is expressly allowed by law.

2. An officer or other person, to whom a fee or other compensation is allowed by law, for any service, shall not charge or receive a greater fee or reward, for that service, than is so allowed.

3. An officer, or other person, shall not demand or receive any fee or compensation, allowed to him by law for any service, unless the service was actually rendered by him;

except that an officer may demand in advance his fee, where he is, by law, expressly directed or permitted to require payment thereof, before rendering the service.

4. An officer or other person, who violates either of the provisions contained in this section, is liable, in addition to the punishment prescribed by law for the criminal offense, to an action in behalf of the person aggrieved, in which the plaintiff is entitled to treble damages.

A notary public subjects himself to criminal prosecution, civil suit and possible removal by asking or receiving more than the statutory allowance, for administering the ordinary oath in connect with an affidavit. (Op. Atty. Gen. (1917) 12 St. Dept. Rep. 507.)

SUMMARY

1. A public officer who has a duty expressly imposed by law must do so without fee or reward, unless the law allows such.

2. When a fee is allowed, a public officer may not charge more than what is allowed.

3. A person shall not request any fee unless the service has been provided by him, but may demand the fee in advance when the law allows so.

4. A person who violates this section is liable for treble damages, as well as criminal liability.

A notary public subjects himself to criminal prosecution, civil suit, and removal by asking or receiving a higher fee than allowed for administering the ordinary oath with an affidavit.

TRUE OR FALSE?

40. If the law allows it, a public officer may demand a fee before a duty is performed.

✓ Answer key on Page 130

Section 69 - Fee for administering certain official oaths prohibited

An officer is not entitled to a fee, for administering the oath of office to a member of the legislature, to any military officer, to an inspector of election, clerk of the poll, or to any other public officer or public employee.

SUMMARY

An officer is not entitled to a fee for administering an oath of office to any public officer or public employee.

TRUE OR FALSE?

41. An officer may collect $2 for administering an oath of office to a member of the legislature.

✓ Answer key on Page 130

EXECUTIVE LAW

Misconduct by a notary and removal from office

A notary public who, in the performance of the duties of such office shall practice any fraud or deceit, is guilty of a misdemeanor (Executive Law, Section 135-a), and may be removed from office. The notary may be removed from office if the notary made a misstatement of a material fact in his application for appointment; for preparing and taking an oath of an affiant to a statement that the notary knew to be false or fraudulent.

SUMMARY

Any notary who, while using his powers practices fraud or deceit, will be guilty of a misdemeanor and may be removed from office.

TRUE OR FALSE?

42. A notary public taking an oath of an affiant to a statement that the did not know to be false has committed a misdemeanor.

✓ Answer key on Page 130

PENAL LAW

Section 70.00 - Sentence of imprisonment for felony

2. Maximum term of sentence. The maximum term of an indeterminate sentence shall be at least three years and the term shall be fixed as follows:

d. For a class D felony, the term shall be fixed by the court, and shall not exceed 7 years; and
e. For a class E felony, the term shall be fixed by the court, and shall not exceed 4 years.

SUMMARY

2. The maximum term of an indefinite sentence is at least 3 years, and fixed as follows:
    d. For a class D felony, shall not exceed 7 years; and
    e. For a class E felony, shall not exceed 4 years.

TRUE OR FALSE?

43. A felony imprisonment should not exceed 5 years.

✓ Answer key on Page 130

Section 70.15 - Sentences of imprisonment for misdemeanors and violation

1. Class A misdemeanor. A sentence of imprisonment for a class A misdemeanor shall be a definite sentence. When such a sentence is imposed the term shall be fixed by the court, and shall not exceed one year.

SUMMARY

A sentence of imprisonment for a class A misdemeanor shall be a fixed sentence, and shall not exceed 1 year.

TRUE OR FALSE?

44. Misdemeanors imprisonments should not exceed 1 year.

✓ Answer key on Page 130

Section 170.10 - Forgery in the second degree

A person is guilty of forgery in the second degree when, with intent to defraud, deceive or injure another, he falsely makes, completes or alters a written instrument which is or purports to be, or which is calculated to become or to represent if completed:

1. A deed, will, codicil, contract, assignment, commercial instrument, or other instrument which does or may evidence, create, transfer, terminate or otherwise affect a legal right, interest, obligation or status; or

2. A public record, or an instrument filed or required or authorized by law to be filed in or with a public office or public servant; or

3. A written instrument officially issued or created by a public office, public servant or governmental instrumentality.

Forgery in the second degree is a class D felony.

SUMMARY

A person is guilty of forgery in the second degree when he intends to deceive or injure another, or if he falsely makes or alters the following written instruments:

1. A deed, will, contract, or any instrument that creates, transfers, or terminates a legal right; or

2. A public record, or an instrument to be filed in a public office or with a public servant; or

3. A written instrument created by a public office or public servant.

Forgery in the second degree is a class D felony.

TRUE OR FALSE?

45. Forgery is a class E felony.

✓ Answer key on Page 130

Section 175.40 - Issuing a false certificate

A person is guilty of issuing a false certificate when, being a public servant authorized by law to make or issue official certificates or other official written instruments, and with intent to defraud, deceive or injure another person, he issues such an instrument, or makes the same with intent that it be issued, knowing that it contains a false statement or false information.

Issuing a false certificate is a class E felony.

SUMMARY

A public servant is guilty of issuing false certificates when he is authorized by law to make official certificates, has the intent to defraud, deceive, or injure another person, and knows that it has false statements or information.

This is a class E felony.

TRUE OR FALSE?

46. Issuing a false certificate is a class E Felony.

✓ Answer key on Page 130

Section 195.00 - Official misconduct

A public servant is guilty of official misconduct when, with intent to obtain a benefit or to injure or deprive another person of a benefit:

1. He commits an act relating to his office but constituting an unauthorized exercise of his official functions, knowing that such act is unauthorized; or

2. He knowingly refrains from performing a duty which is imposed upon him by law or is clearly inherent in the nature of his office. Official misconduct is a class A misdemeanor.

SUMMARY

A public servant is guilty of misconduct when, with intent to benefit or injure:

   d. Commits an act relating to his office but is an unauthorized exercise of his powers, while knowing so.

   e. Knowingly refrains from performing his duty that is imposed by law or clearly inherent.

Official misconduct is a class A misdemeanor.

TRUE OR FALSE?

47. Official misconduct is a Class D felony.

✓ Answer key on Page 130

Notary must officiate on request

The Penal Law (§195.00) provides that an officer before whom an oath or affidavit may be taken is bound to administer the same when requested, and a refusal to do so is a misdemeanor. (People v. Brooks, 1 Den. 457.)

SUMMARY

A notary public is legally required to perform their duties when asked. If they refuse, it is considered a minor criminal offense (misdemeanor).

TRUE OR FALSE?

48. It's a criminal offense for a notary public to refuse to carry out their notarization duties when requested.

✓ Answer key on Page 130

Perjury

One is guilty of perjury if he has stated or given testimony on a material matter, under oath or by affirmation, as to the truth thereof, when he knew the statement or testimony to be false and willfully made.

SUMMARY

Perjury occurs when an individual intentionally makes a false statement while under oath or affirmation.

TRUE OR FALSE?

49. Perjury involves making an unintentional false statement under oath.

✓ Answer key on Page 130

Section 182.1 - Advertising

a. A notary public who is not an attorney licensed to practice law in the State of New York shall not falsely advertise that he or she is an attorney licensed to practice law in the State of New York or in any jurisdiction of the United States by using foreign terms including, but not limited to: abogado, mandataire, procuratore, Адвокат, 律師, and avoca.

b. A notary public who is not an attorney licensed to practice law in the State of New York and who advertises his or her services as a notary public in a language other than English shall include in the advertisement the following disclaimer:

"I am not an attorney licensed to practice law and may not give legal advice about immigration or any other legal matter or accept fees for legal advice."

The disclaimer shall be printed clearly and conspicuously and shall be made in the same language as the advertisement. The translated disclaimer, in some but not all languages, is as follows:

1. Simplified Chinese:
我不是有执照的律师，不能出庭辩护，不能提供有关移民事务或 其他法律事务的法律建议，也不能收取法律咨询的费用。

2. Traditional Chinese:
本人不是持牌執業律師，因此不能出庭辯護,不能向閣下提供移民 及其他法律事務方面的法律意見，也不能收取法律諮詢費

3. Spanish:
"No estoy facultado para ejercer la profesión de abogado y no puedo brindar asesoría legal sobre inmigración o ningún otro asunto legal como tampoco puedo cobrar honorarios por la asesoría legal."

4. Korean:
저는 법을 집행할 수 있는 자격이 있는 변호사가 아니며, 이민이나 또는 다른 적법한 문제나 혹은 적법한 조언에 대한 수수료를 받을 수 있는지에 대한 법률상의 조언을 드릴수 가 없을지도 모릅니다.

5. Haitian Creole:
MWEN PA AVOKA KI GEN LISANS POU PRATIKE LWA E MWEN PA KA BAY KONSÈY LEGAL SOU ZAFÈ IMIGRASYON OSWA NENPÒT KI LÒT ZAFÈ LEGAL OSWA AKSEPTE LAJEN POU BAY KONSÈY LEGAL.

SUMMARY

a. A notary public who is not an attorney shall not falsely advertise that they are an attorney by using foreign terms.

b. A notary public who advertises in a foreign language other than English shall include the following disclaimer, clearly and obviously in the same foreign language used:

"I am not an attorney licensed to practice law and may not give legal advice about immigration or any other legal matter or accept fees for legal advice."

TRUE OR FALSE?

50. A notary public who is not an attorney needs to include a disclaimer on any advertisement in any language.

✓ Answer key on Page 130

182.2 Definitions

For purposes of this Part, the following terms have the following meanings:
a. "Notary Public" or "Notary" means an individual who meets the qualifications set forth in section 130 of the Executive Law and has been appointed by the secretary of state pursuant to section 131 of the Executive Law to perform notarial acts in accordance with procedures outlined in article 6 of the Executive Law and this Part.

b. "Electronic notary public" or "electronic notary" means a notary public or notary who has registered with the secretary of state the capability of performing electronic notarial acts in accordance with section 135-c of the Executive Law and this Part.

c. "Notarial act" means any official act that a notary public is authorized to perform by law, including, but not limited to:
   1. administering oaths and affirmations;
   2. taking affidavits and depositions;
   3. receiving and certifying acknowledgments or proof of such written instruments as deeds, mortgages, powers of attorney and other instruments in writing;
   4. demanding acceptance or payment of foreign and inland bills of exchange, promissory notes and obligations in writing, and protesting the same for non-acceptance or non-payment, as the case may require;
   5. preparation of a certificate of authenticity in accordance with paragraph (d) of subdivision six of section 135-c of the Executive Law or
   6. an electronic notarial act.

d. "Electronic notarial act" means an official act by a notary public, physically present in the state of New York, on or involving an electronic record and using communication technology authorized by this Part.

e. "Record" means information that is inscribed on a tangible medium or stored in an electronic or other medium and is retrievable in perceivable form. The term "record" includes an electronic record.

f. "Electronic record" means information that is created, generated, sent, communicated, received, or stored by electronic means.

g. "Identity verification" means the use of an authentication process by which a notary public validates the identity of any principal and/or individual present for a notarial act.

h. "Credential analysis" means a process or service operating according to the standards adopted in this Part, through which a third-party affirms the validity of government-issued identification through review of public and proprietary data sources.

i. "Credential service provider" means a third party trusted entity that issues or registers subscriber authenticators and issues electronic credentials to subscribers.

j. "Identity proofing" means a process by which a credential service provider collects, validates, and verifies information about a person.

k. "Personal appearance" means presence at a transaction for which a notarial act is required, either physically or electronically, in a manner that meets all requirements imposed by this Part.

l. "Communication technology" means an electronic device or process that: (1) allows a notary public and a remotely located individual to communicate with each other simultaneously by sight and sound; and (2) when necessary and consistent with other applicable law, facilitates communication with a remotely located individual who has a vision, hearing, or speech impairment.

m. "Electronic signature" has the same meaning set forth in subdivision 3 of section 302 of the State Technology Law, except that any electronic signature affixed by an electronic notary in the performance of an electronic notarial act must also meet the additional requirements outlined in this Part.

n. "Public key infrastructure" means the architecture, organization, techniques, practices, and procedures that collectively support the implementation and operation of a certificate-based asymmetric or public/private key cryptographic system.

o. "Public/private key or asymmetric cryptographic system" means a system by which two mathematically linked keys are generated, one a publicly available validation key and the other a private key that cannot be deduced from the public key.

p. "Principal" means an individual:
   1. whose signature is reflected on a record that is notarized;
   2. who has taken an oath or affirmation administered by a notary public;
   3. whose signature is reflected on a record that is notarized after the individual has taken an oath or affirmation administered by a notary public; or
   4. for purposes of this Part, any individual who intends to engage in any of these acts.

SUMMARY

a. A "Notary Public" or "Notary" is someone qualified and appointed by the secretary of state to carry out notarial acts.

b. An "Electronic notary public" or "electronic notary" is a notary who can perform notarial acts electronically after registering with the secretary of state.

c. "Notarial act" includes a range of official acts a notary is allowed to do, like administering oaths, certifying documents, and protesting unpaid bills.

d. An "Electronic notarial act" is an official act by a notary on an electronic document while in New York, using approved communication technology.

e. "Record" refers to information written on something tangible or stored electronically that can be retrieved and understood.

f. "Electronic record" is information created or stored electronically.

g. "Identity verification" is when a notary confirms the identity of a person present for a notarial act.

h. "Credential analysis" is a third-party process that checks the validity of government-issued IDs.

i. "Credential service provider" is a trusted third party that gives electronic credentials and registers them.

j. "Identity proofing" is when a provider checks and verifies personal information about a person.

k. "Personal appearance" means being present, either physically or electronically, for a notarial act in a way that meets legal requirements.

l. "Communication technology" is an electronic method allowing notaries and individuals to see and hear each other at the same time and assists individuals with impairments when necessary.

m. "Electronic signature" is defined in the State Technology Law and for electronic notaries, it must meet extra requirements.

n. "Public key infrastructure" involves the support systems for a cryptographic system that uses a certificate-based public/private key.

o. "Public/private key or asymmetric cryptographic system" generates two mathematically related keys: one public for validation, and one private.

p. "Principal" is the person signing a record or taking an oath before a notary, or any individual intending to perform these acts.

TRUE OR FALSE?

51. A New York notary public can perform electronic notarial acts even if they are not physically present in the state of New York at the time of the notarization.

✓ Answer key on Page 130

182.3 Requirements for Notaries

a. All notaries public who wish to perform notarial acts in New York State, must:
   1. satisfy the requirements of sections 130 and 131 of the Executive Law;
   2. obtain satisfactory evidence of the identity of any principal or other individual appearing before the notary in a manner authorized by this Part;
   3. require the personal appearance of all parties to any transaction for which a notarial act is required for the duration of any such transaction, except acts performed as authorized and in conformity with this Part and section 135-c of Executive Law unless a law expressly excludes such authorization;
   4. administer any oath or affirmation as required by the law governing the transaction for which the notarial act is required and, regardless of the county of qualification, include and affix to each instrument requiring an oath or affirmation such notary public's official number;

5. disqualify themselves from performing notarial acts for transactions in which the notary is a party or directly and pecuniarily interested in the transaction;
6. refuse to perform a notarial act when the requirements of this Part are not met, or if the notary is not satisfied that the official record or the presented record evidences the individual's capacity to act as the representative on the record presented for notarization;
7. maintain records as required by this Part; and
8. within five days after a change of name, address, or e-mail address, transmit to the secretary of state a notice of the change, signed with the notary public's official signature.

b. A notary may refuse to perform a notarial act if the notary public is not satisfied that:
1. the principal is competent or has the capacity to execute a record; and/or
2. the principal's signature is knowingly and voluntarily made.

SUMMARY

a. Rules for Notaries in New York:
1. Meet the qualifications according to the Executive Law sections 130 and 131;
2. Verify the identity of anyone involved in a notarial act as authorized;
3. Ensure all parties are present for the entire transaction, unless specific laws allow otherwise;
4. Administer oaths or affirmations as required by law and include the notary's official number on document;
5. Avoid notarizing transactions where the notary has a personal or financial interest;
6. Refuse notarization if the part's requirements aren't met or if the notary doubts the person's authority or capacity;
7. Keep required records of notarizations; and
8. Notify the secretary of state within five days of any changes to name, address, or email, using their official signature.

b. Notary's Right to Refuse:
1. A notary can refuse to notarize if they doubt the principal's competence or capacity; and/or
2. A notary can refuse if they believe the principal's signature isn't voluntary.

TRUE OR FALSE?

52. A notary public in New York is required to update their official records with the secretary of state within five days following any change to their name, address, or email.

✓ Answer key on Page 130

182.4 Additional Requirements for Electronic Notaries

a. In addition to the requirements set forth in section 182.3 of this Part, all notaries public who wish to perform electronic notarial acts in New York State must:
1. register the capability to notarize electronically with the secretary of state in compliance with this Part;
2. use only those vendors or providers who comply with the standards outlined in this Part and any communication or reporting relating to those standards as
3. required by the secretary of state;
4. be physically located within the boundaries of New York when performing electronic notarial acts;
5. use a network that permits location detection when performing an electronic notarial act, meaning that no action, process or device shall be used to disguise or hide the actual location from which the electronic notary is performing the electronic notarial act, and that no function on any system or device used by an electronic notary that permits location detection shall be disabled or otherwise interfered with during the performance of an electronic notarial act;
6. affix a reliable electronic signature to electronic records. An electronic signature is reliable if it is:
   i. unique to the notary public;

   ii. attached or logically associated with an electronic record by use of a digital certificate that utilizes public key infrastructure as defined in this Part and is capable of independent verification;
   iii. retained under the notary's sole control; and
   iv. linked to the data in such a manner that any subsequent alterations to the underlying record are detectable and may invalidate the electronic notarial act;
7. use their designated electronic signature only for the purpose of performing electronic notarial acts or as otherwise specified in this Part;
8. ensure the remote online notarial certificate for an electronic notarial act clearly states that the person making the acknowledgement or making the oath appeared using communication technology;
9. for execution of any instrument in writing, if under applicable law the record may be signed with an electronic signature, confirm that such instrument is the same instrument in which the principal made a statement or on which the principal executed a signature;
10. if the principal is located outside of the United States, verify, through verbal confirmation made by the principal in the course of the recorded electronic notarial act, that the record or subject of the notarial act:

i. is to be filed with or relates to a matter before a public official or court, governmental entity, or other entity subject to the jurisdiction of the United States; or
ii. involves property located in the territorial jurisdiction of the United States or involves a transaction substantially connected with the United States;
11. In complying with paragraph (8) of subdivision (a) of section 182.3 of this Part ensure that the notice of change is electronically transmitted to the secretary of state, signed with the notary public's designated electronic signature;
12. for any update to the information required to be submitted by a notary public to register the capability to perform an electronic notarial act, make such update prior to performance of any electronic notarial act; and

b. The notary public shall not disclose any access information used to affix the electronic notary's signature and seal except when requested by the secretary of state or a designee, or judicial subpoena, and with reasonable precautions, electronic document preparation and transmission vendors. Control of security aspects such as but not limited to passwords, token devices, biometrics, PINS, phrases, software on protected hardware shall remain under the sole control of the notary public.

SUMMARY

a. Additional requirements for Electronic Notarization in New York:
1. Register for electronic notarization with the secretary of state;
2. Work only with approved vendors that meet state standards;
3. Be physically in New York when performing electronic notarizations;
4. Use a network that accurately shows the notary's location without interference;
5. Securely affix a unique electronic signature that meets specific security standards;
6. Use the electronic signature solely for notarial acts or as allowed by regulations;
7. Clearly indicate the use of communication technology in the notarial certificate;
8. Verify that electronically signed documents are the same ones the principal has signed;
9. Confirm that notarizations involving a principal outside the U.S. are connected to U.S. jurisdictions or involve U.S. property or transactions;
10. Electronically submit any changes to notary information using the designated electronic signature;
11. Update registration information before performing further electronic notarial acts; and

b. Privacy and Security for Notaries: Notaries must keep their electronic signature and seal access information confidential, sharing only when legally required or with appropriate precautions..

TRUE OR FALSE?

53. A notary public performing electronic notarial acts in New York can use any electronic signature, regardless of the security features or technology it employs

✓ *Answer key on Page 130*

182.5 Satisfactory Evidence of Identity

a. For any individual signing a document who makes a personal appearance before a notary public, including but not limited to any principal seeking a notarial act, and any witness thereto, the notary must obtain satisfactory evidence of the identity of each such individual that complies with the requirements of this Part.

b. For any individual signing a document who physically appears before a notary public, satisfactory evidence of identity requires identity verification through:
   1. presentation of the back and front of an identification card issued by a governmental agency provided the card:
      i. is valid and current;
      ii. contains the photographic image of the bearer;
      iii. has an accurate physical description of the bearer, if applicable; and
      iv. includes the signature of the bearer;
   2. at least two current documents issued by an institution, business entity, or federal or state government with at least the individual's signature;
   3. attestation by the notary that the individual is personally known to them;
   4. the oath or affirmation of a witness who is personally known to both the individual and notary; or
   5. the oath or affirmation of two witnesses who know the individual personally and provide identification that meets the requirements of paragraph (1) of subdivision (b) of this section.

c. For any individual signing a document who appears before an electronic notary public using communication technology, and who is not personally known to the notary public, satisfactory evidence of identity requires all of the following:
   1. identity verification as outlined in subdivision (b) of this section, utilizing communication technology that meets the requirements set forth in this Part;
   2. credential analysis that meets the requirements set forth in this Part; and
   3. identity proofing by a third-party service provider that meets the requirements set forth in this Part.

d. Provided that all other requirements of this Part are met, attestation by an electronic notary public that an individual appearing through communication technology is personally known to them is satisfactory evidence of identity for electronic notarial acts.

SUMMARY

a. Notaries must verify the identity of every person who appears before them for a notarization, including principals and witnesses, according to the rules of this Part.

b. For in-person notarizations, identity can be proven by:
   1. A government-issued ID card that is current, has a photo, physical description, and the person's signature.
   2. Two documents with the individual's signature from credible institutions or governments.
   3. The notary's personal knowledge of the individual.
   4. The sworn statement of a mutual acquaintance of the notary and the individual.
   5. The sworn statements of two acquaintances who know the individual and have proper ID themselves.

c. For electronic notarizations when the notary does not personally know the individual, identity must be proven with:
   1. Identity verification using approved technology.
   2. Credential analysis according to this Part's standards.
   3. Identity proofing by a third-party service that complies with this Part.

d. For electronic notarizations, if all other rules are met, a notary can attest to knowing the individual personally as sufficient evidence for the notarial act.

TRUE OR FALSE?

54. When conducting an electronic notarization, if a notary public personally knows the individual, they do not need to follow any other identity verification procedures.

✓ Answer key on Page 130

182.6 Credential Analysis

Credential analysis must conform to all standards set forth in this section.

a. Credential analysis must be performed by a third-party service provider who has provided evidence to the online notary public of the provider's ability to satisfy the requirements set forth in this rule.

b. Credential analysis must utilize public or private data sources to confirm the validity of an identification credential and must, at a minimum:
   1. use automated software processes to aid the online notary public in verifying the identity of a remotely located individual;
   2. ensure that the identification credential passes an authenticity test, consistent with sound commercial practices that:
      i. uses technologies consistent with the requirements of this Part to confirm the integrity of visual, physical, or cryptographic security features;
      ii. uses technologies consistent with the requirements of this Part to confirm that the identification credential is not fraudulent or inappropriately modified;
      iii. uses information held or published by the issuing source or an authoritative source, as available, to confirm the validity of identification credential details; and
      iv. provides output of the authenticity test to the online notary public.

SUMMARY

a. A third-party service must conduct the credential analysis for online notarization, and they must prove their capability to the notary.

b. The credential analysis process must:
   1. Utilize software to help the notary verify the identity of the person notarizing remotely.
   2. Check that the ID credential is authentic, using:
      i. Technology approved by this rule to check the ID's security features.
      ii. Technology approved by this rule to make sure the ID hasn't been tampered with or is fake.
      iii. Confirmation from the issuing or an authoritative source to validate the ID details.
      iv. Give the notary the results of the ID check.

TRUE OR FALSE?

55. Credential analysis for online notarization must include an authenticity test that checks the ID against data from the issuing source or an authoritative source to confirm its validity.

✓ Answer key on Page 130

182.7 Identity Proofing

a. Identity proofing must meet, at minimum, the Identity Assurance Level 2 standard as outlined in the Digital Identity Guidelines of the National Institute of Standards and Technology, as referenced in subdivision (b) of this section, or any industry accepted standard that is at least as secure, or more secure, than that standard.

b. Incorporation by reference. The Identity Assurance Level 2 standard, as outlined in the Digital Identity Guidelines of the National Institute of Standards and Technology, United States Department of Commerce, document SP 800-63-3, Revision 3, dated June 2017 and includes updates as of 03-02-2020, is hereby incorporated by reference. This publication is available free of charge from:
https://doi.org/10.6028/NIST.SP.800-63-3

Copies of said publication may be obtained from the publisher at the following address:
National Institute of Standards and Technology
Attn: Applied Cybersecurity Division, Information Technology Laboratory
100 Bureau Drive (Mail Stop 2000) Gaithersburg, MD 20899-2000
Email: dig-comments@nist.gov

Copies of said publication are available for public inspection and copying at the Office of the New York State Department of State located at One Commerce Plaza, 99 Washington Avenue, Albany, NY 12231-0001.

SUMMARY

a. Identity proofing for notarization must adhere to the Identity Assurance Level 2 standard from the National Institute of Standards and Technology's Digital Identity Guidelines or an equivalent or higher industry standard.

b. Reference Information:
- The specific guidelines (SP 800-63-3, Revision 3, as updated until 03-02-2020) are included by reference and can be accessed online without charge.
- Physical copies can be requested from the National Institute of Standards and Technology's Applied Cybersecurity Division.
- These guidelines are also available for public review at the New York State Department of State's office.

TRUE OR FALSE?

56. For identity proofing in notarization, standards lower than the Identity Assurance Level 2 as outlined by the National Institute of Standards and Technology are acceptable.

✓ *Answer key on Page 130*

182.8 Communication Technology

a. The communication technology used to perform electronic notarial acts must:
   1. permit sufficient audio and visual clarity to enable the notary and the person(s) for whom a notarial act is requested to see and speak to each other simultaneously through live, real-time transmission throughout the duration of the notarial act, through and including identity verification, identity proofing, the signature of any parties present during the transaction and the application of the notary's signature and seal without interruption;
   2. permit sufficient visual clarity to enable the notary to view, read, and capture the front and back of any identification card presented as verification of identity;
   3. include a signal transmission secure from interception through lawful means by anyone other than the parties to the notarial act;
   4. include a process of reproduction that does not permit additions, deletions, or changes without leaving a record of such additions, deletions, or changes;
   5. provide some manner of ensuring that the electronic record that is presented for electronic notarization is the same record electronically signed by the principal; and
   6. permit recording and archiving of the audio-video communication session as required by subdivision (b) of this section.

b. The electronic notary shall keep a copy of the recording of the video and audio conference that includes at minimum:
   1. the complete notarial act, including the verification required by paragraph 9 of subdivision (a) of section 182.4 of this Part;
   2. any signatures required for completion of the notarial act; and
   3. a verbal description of the type of identification used.

SUMMARY

a. The electronic tools used for online notarization must:
   1. Provide clear audio and video for the notary and participants to interact in real time, from identity checks to signing documents.
   2. Allow the notary to clearly see and record both sides of any ID card used for proving identity.
   3. Protect the communication from being intercepted by anyone not part of the notarial act.

4. Record the process in such a way that any changes to the document are traceable and no unauthorized alterations can be made without detection.
5. Ensure the document being notarized electronically is the same one signed by the person requesting notarization.
6. Enable the notarization session, including audio and video, to be recorded and stored as per the regulations.

b. Notaries must save the video and audio recording of the notarization session, which should include:
   1. The entire process of notarization, along with identity verification as specified in the regulations.
   2. All signatures made during the notarization.
   3. A spoken account of the type of ID used for verifying the signer's identity.

TRUE OR FALSE?

57. The communication technology used for electronic notarial acts must be capable of recording any changes made to the document during the notarization process.

✓ Answer key on Page 130

182.9 Recordkeeping and Reporting

a. In addition to any required video and audio conference recording, all notaries public must maintain records sufficient to document compliance with the requirements of sections 130 and 135-c of the Executive Law and the duties and responsibilities of a notary public and/or electronic notary public as outlined in this Part. Record storage may be made through a third party if safeguarded through a password or other secure means of authentication or access. Such records shall be made contemporaneously with the performance of the notarial act and must include:
   1. the date, approximate time, and type of notarial acts performed;
   2. the name and address of any individuals for whom a notarial act was performed;
   3. the number and type of notarial services provided;
   4. the type of credential used to identify the principal, including, for verification made in accordance with paragraphs (4) or (5) of subdivision (b) of section 182.5, the names of the witnesses and, if applicable, the type of credential used;
   5. the verification procedures used for any personal appearance before the notary public; and
   6. for electronic notarial acts, identification of the communication technology and, if not included as part of the communication technology used by the electronic notary, the certification authority and verification providers used.

b. Any records maintained by a notary public pursuant to this Part must be retained by the notary public for at least ten years.

c. Any records retained by a notary public pursuant to this Part must be capable of being produced to the secretary of state and others as necessary in relation to the performance of the notary public's obligations pursuant to the Executive Law and this Part.

SUMMARY

a. Notaries must keep detailed records to show they're following legal requirements and notary duties. These records can be stored via a third party, but must be protected with secure access. Records should be created at the time of the notarization and include:
2. The date, time, and type of notarial act.
3. The names and addresses of the people involved in the notarial act.
4. How many and what types of notarizations were done.
5. The ID used to verify the principal, and the names and IDs of any witnesses if used.
6. The methods used to confirm the identity of individuals appearing before the notary.
7. For electronic notarizations, details of the technology used, and the authorities and providers for identity verification.

b. Notaries must keep these records for at least ten years.

c. The records must be accessible for review by the secretary of state or other relevant authorities concerning the notary's professional responsibilities.

TRUE OR FALSE?

58. A notary public can discard the records of notarization after five years.

✓ Answer key on Page 130

182.10 Applications, Registrations and Renewals

a. Prior to performing any notarial acts, a notary public must be appointed and commissioned by the secretary of state for a four-year term in accordance with the requirements and procedures set forth in Executive Law sections 130 and 131 and must provide all information required by the application form prescribed by the secretary of state.

b. No commissioned notary public may perform electronic notarial acts until they have registered the capability to notarize electronically on a form prescribed the secretary of state, including, in addition to any other information prescribed by the secretary of state, the following information:
   1. the notary's name as currently commissioned and complete mailing address:
   2. the expiration date of the notary's commission and signature of the commissioned notary;
   3. the notary's email address;
   4. the description of the electronic technology or technologies to be used in attaching the notary's electronic signature to the electronic record, which may be effectuated by registration of vendor account information from a vendor who meets the requirements of this Part, in the manner required by the department of state;
   5. an exemplar of the notary's electronic signature, which shall be provided through and in the manner required by the department of state's registration system using the notary's selected signature vendor and shall contain the notary's name and any necessary instructions, authorizations, or techniques that allow the notary's electronic signature to be read and verified.

c. A notary public may apply for reappointment within 90 days of expiration of their commission, provided that the notary public continues to meet the requirements set forth in sections 130 and 131 of the Executive Law and this Part.

d. When any notary public who has registered to perform electronic notarial acts applies for reappointment, the electronic notary public must provide verification of the accuracy of all information on file with the secretary of state and affirm that such notary public is otherwise in compliance with all requirements of this Part.

e. Any notary public who has failed to comply with any of the requirements of this Part relating to notarial or electronic notarial acts shall not be eligible for reappointment.

f. All applications for appointment and reappointment of notaries public, and all registrations of capability to perform electronic notarial acts, shall be in the form and manner prescribed by the secretary of state and provided through the department of state's division of licensing.

SUMMARY

a. Before doing any notary work, a person must be officially appointed by the secretary of state for four years, as detailed in the Executive Law, and must fill out the required application form.

b. Notaries can't perform electronic notarizations until they've registered this ability with the secretary of state. The registration must include:
   2. The notary's legal name, address, and commission expiration date.
   3. The notary's signature.
   4. Their email address.
   5. Details about the technology they'll use for electronic signatures.
   6. A sample of their electronic signature, made using approved vendor technology.

a. Notaries can apply for a new term 90 days before their current one ends, as long as they still meet all the legal requirements.

b. Electronic notaries must confirm their information is correct and they're following all rules when they reapply.

c. Notaries who haven't followed the rules for notarizations aren't allowed to reapply.

d. All applications and registrations for notaries, including those for electronic notarization, must be done as specified by the secretary of state and through the state's licensing department.

TRUE OR FALSE?

59. Notaries public must include a sample of their electronic signature when registering to perform electronic notarial acts.

✓ Answer key on Page 130

182.11 Fees

a. Applicants for a notary public commission must submit a non-refundable application fee of sixty dollars, which fee shall be used and distributed in accordance with section 131 of the Executive Law.

b. Registrants for electronic notarial acts must submit a non-refundable registration fee of sixty dollars to the secretary of state with their registration.

c. Notaries public who wish to renew their notary public commission must pay a non-refundable fee of sixty dollars, which fee shall be used and distributed in accordance with section 131 of the Executive Law.

d. Notary Public applicants who must take a written exam must submit a fee of fifteen dollars for each examination taken, payable on the date of the examination.

e. The fee for change requests and Duplicate License/Registration Requests shall be ten dollars, payable to the secretary of state at the time of submission of the request.

f. A notary public shall be entitled to a fee for notarial acts as set forth in section 136 of the Executive Law.

g. An electronic notary public shall be entitled to a fee of twenty-five dollars for each electronic notarial act performed, which shall be inclusive of all costs incurred by the notary public.

h. All application, renewal, and registration fees required to be paid pursuant to this section shall be transmitted in a manner prescribed by the secretary of state.

SUMMARY

a. Applying for a notary public commission costs a non-refundable fee of $60, as directed by Executive Law section 131.

b. Those registering for electronic notarization must pay a non-refundable fee of $60.

c. Notaries renewing their commission must also pay a non-refundable fee of $60, used as specified in section 131 of the Executive Law.

d. Applicants required to take a written exam must pay $15 for each attempt, paid on the exam day.

e. Requests for changes or duplicate licenses/registrations cost $10 each, payable upon request submission.

f. Notaries can charge fees for their services as outlined in section 136 of the Executive Law.

g. Electronic notaries can charge $25 for each electronic notarization, covering all incurred costs.

i. Fees for applications, renewals, and registrations must be sent as the secretary of state specifies.

TRUE OR FALSE?

60. An electronic notary public can charge more than $25 for each electronic notarial act if additional costs are incurred.

✓ Answer key on Page 130

DEFINITIONS AND GENERAL TERMS

Acknowledgment

A formal declaration made before an officer (i.e. notary public) by a person who has executed a written instrument as his free act and deed.

A notary public should not take an acknowledgment if he has an interest in the legal instrument.

A notary public who makes a false certificate is guilty of forgery in the second degree. It is punishable by imprisonment for a term of not exceeding 7 years.

A notary public taking acknowledgments over the telephone is guilty of a misdemeanor.

Administrator

A person appointed by the court to manage the estate of a deceased person who left no will.

Affiant

The person who swears to an affidavit.

Affidavit

A sworn statement signed by the person swearing by it. It is sworn personally before a notary public or other officer who has the authority to administer an oath.

An affidavit is an ex parte statement.

Affirmation

Someone who declines to take an oath for religious, ethical, or other reasons. Instead of taking an oath, the person may affirm that certain statements are true. It is equivalent to an oath and is just as binding.

Apostile

A form of authentication issued by the Department of State. It is a notarized and county-certified document. Can be used internationally.

Attest

To be present and subscribe as a witness to the execution of a written instrument, at the request of the person who makes it.

Attestation Clause

The clause at the end of a will where the witnesses certify that the will was executed before them, and the manner of the execution of the same.

Authentication (Notarial)

A document signed by a notary public that is authenticated by a county clerk. This authenticates/verifies the authority of the notary public. Also called county clerk's certificate.

Bill of Sale

A written instrument given from a vendor (seller) to a vendee (buyer) to pass the title of personal property.

Certified Copy

A signed and certified public record meant to certify that it is the original copy. Only public officials who have the original copy can perform the certification. A notary public cannot issue certified copies.

Chattel

Movable personal property, such as household goods or fixtures. Does not include real estate.

Chattel Paper

Writing that indicates that the holder is owed money and has a security interest in valuable goods associated with the debt.

Codicil

An instrument made after a will and modifying the will in some respects.

Consideration

Anything of value (i.e. money, possessions, love, etc.) given to initiate a contract.

Contempt of Court

Disrespectful behavior towards the authority of a court that disrupts the execution of court orders.

Contract

An agreement between parties for a legal consideration.

Conveyance (Deed)

A legal document that serves as proof of a deed (or title) that creates, transfers, assigns, or surrenders any estate or interest in real property.

Deponent

A person who testifies to information or facts under oath in a deposition. A deponent is also an affiant.

Deposition

A witness's sworn out-of-court testimony under oath or by affirmation, before an authorized official. It is used at the trial or hearing.

Duress

Unlawful constraint put on a person to be forced to do some act against his will.

Escrow

An instrument that is put into the custody of a third party to be held until the occurrence of an event.

Executor

A person named in a will to carry out the requirements of the will.

Ex Parte (From One Side Only)

A hearing or examination without requiring all of the parties to be present.

Felony

A crime punishable by death or imprisonment in a state prison.

Guardian

A person in charge of a minor's person or property.

Judgment

A decision of a court regarding the rights and liabilities of parties in a legal action or proceeding.

Jurat

The clause at the end of the document stating the date, place, and name of the officer (notary public) certifies that it was sworn to before him.

The following is generally used as a form of jurat:

"Sworn to before me this .... day of ...., 20 ......"

Laches

The delay or negligence in asserting one's legal rights.

Lease

A contract made for a consideration (i.e. rent) in which the owner of property (real estate, car, etc.) allows use of the property for a specified period of time (term).

Lien

The right to retain the possession of another person's property until the owner fulfills a legal duty to the person holding the property, such as satisfying a debt.

Litigation

The act of carrying on a lawsuit.

Misdemeanor

Any crime other than a felony.

Mortgage On Real Property

A legal document that creates a lien on real estate as security until a debt has been satisfied.

Notary Public

A public officer who can perform many duties such as:
- Executes acknowledgments of deeds
- Administer oaths and affirmations of the truthfulness of statements on documents
- Take affidavits declarations

Oath

A declaration made by the person taking it that his statements are true to his knowledge. It must be taken before an authorized person (notary public).

An oath must be administered as required by law personally in front of a notary public and cannot be administered over the telephone.

The person taking the oath must say "I do" or something similar in meaning.

A corporation or a partnership cannot take an oath.

A notary public cannot administer an oath to himself.

Plaintiff

A person or group who initiates a lawsuit against another party.

Power of Attorney

A legal document that gives one person the power to act for another person.

Proof

A formal declaration made by a subscribing witness usually states that he witnessed the signature of the signer of the document.

Protest

A formal declaration made by a notary public declaring a default in payment on a promissory note.

Seal

In NYS, notaries public are not required to use a seal. The only inscription required is the name of the notary and the words "Notary Public for the State of New York."

Signature of Notary Public

A notary public signature must use the name he was appointed. In addition to this, the following must be included:
- Venue
- Name printed, typewritten, or stamped beneath his signature in black ink
- The words "Notary Public State of New York"
- The name of the county in which he is qualified
- The date that his commission expires

Notaries public who marries during their commission may continue to use the name they were using prior to marriage. If the notary public chooses to use their married name instead, they will need to use this format as their signature and seal: name prior to marriage, followed by the married name in parenthesis. When renewing their commission, they can choose to renew under their married name or the name prior to marriage.

A notary public can be appointed under a religious name if he is a member of a religious order.

Statute

A law established by an act of the Legislature.

Statute of Frauds

A state law that refers that certain kinds of contracts must be in writing so that they can be enforceable.

Statute of Limitations

A law that sets a time limit on initiating criminal prosecution or a civil action.

Subordination Clause

A clause in an agreement which states that a future mortgage takes priority over an existing mortgage.

Sunday

A notary public may administer an oath or take an affidavit or acknowledgment on Sunday, but cannot take a deposition in a civil proceeding.

Swear

To take an oath.

Taking an Acknowledgment

A notary public that is taking an acknowledgment needs to certify that the person acknowledging:

1. Tells the notary public that he is the person named in the instrument
2. Has satisfactory evidence of the identity of the person whose acknowledgment is taken.

After the requirements are met, the notary public certifies the acknowledgment by signing his official signature on the form.

Venue

The location where the notarial act takes place, usually stated in the following format at the beginning of the notarial certificate or at the top of the notary's jurat or official certification:

"State of New York, County of (New York) ss.:"

Will

An instrument by which a person makes a disposition of his property to take effect after death.

SCHEDULE OF FEES

Description	Fee ($)
Appointment as Notary Public- Total Commission Fee ($40 appointment and $20 filing of Oath of Office)	60.00
Change of Name/Address	10.00
Duplicate Identification Card	10.00
Issuance of Certificate of Official Character	1.00
Filing Certificate of Official Character	1.00
Authentication Certificate	3.00
Protest of Note, Commercial Paper, etc.	0.75
Each additional Notice of Protest (limit 5) each	0.10
Oath or Affirmation	2.00
Acknowledgment (each person)	2.00
Proof of Execution (each person)	2.00
Swearing Witness	2.00

TEST-TAKING STRATEGIES

MAKE PREDICTIONS

Your mind is typically the most focused immediately after you have read the question. Try predicting the answer right before reading the answer choices. This technique is useful on questions that test objective factual knowledge. By predicting the answer before reading the available choices, you eliminate the possibility of distraction or being led astray by an incorrect answer choice. Scan the answers to see if your prediction is one of the choices. If it is, you can be confident that you have the right answer. You will feel more confident in your selection if you read the question, predict the answer, and then find your prediction among the answer choices. Be sure to still read all of the answer choices carefully and completely.

ANSWER THE QUESTION

Test authors create some excellent answer choices that are wrong. Don't pick an answer just because it sounds right or you believe it to be true. It MUST answer the question. Don't choose an answer that is factually true but is an incorrect choice because it does not answer the question. Once you've made your selection, go back and check it against the question and make sure you didn't misread the question, and that your choice does answer the question posed. For instance, a test author might turn the question into a negative redirect the focus of the question right at the end. Avoid falling into these traps by reading the answer choices carefully.

PROCESS OF ELIMINATION

The first step in answering long and complicated questions is to make sure you understand what the question is asking. Sometimes it helps to rephrase the question into a statement, or a simpler question. Once you're sure you know what the question is asking, you'll want to begin by eliminating any answer choices that are clearly wrong. Even if doing so only eliminates one out of four or five answer choices, you've still improved your odds of choosing the correct answer choice.

DIFFICULT QUESTIONS

As much as you have prepared to take the test, it is likely that you will come across a few questions for which you simply don't know the answer. In this situation, don't waste too much time on questions that appear too hard or difficult. Follow the process of elimination stated above to try to identify any obviously incorrect answers and guess at the remaining answer choices before giving up. Carefully think about each possible choice independently from the other choices. Ask yourself if it is possible that it could be the correct answer. When going through each choice this way, you are often able to discover things you might have overlooked. After eliminating obviously wrong answers, make a selection and move on to the next question.

CONFUSING ANSWER CHOICES

There may be a tendency to focus on answer choices that are easiest to comprehend. Many people gravitate to these answer choices because they require less concentration. This is a mistake. Many people fall into this trap designed by test authors. It may be difficult to identify so read through each answer choice carefully. Give these types of questions extra attention. When you come across a confusing answer choice, you should give it extra attention. Try to make sense of it. If it is still confusing, set it aside and examine the remaining choices. If you are confident that another answer choice is the correct answer, you can leave the confusing answer choice aside. Otherwise, try rephrasing the confusing answer choice to make sense of it in the context of the question.

DIFFICULT WORDS

Don't choose an answer choice just because it is the only one word you recognize. If you only recognize the words in one answer choice and not the rest, make sure it is correct and really answers the question before you choose it. If you can eliminate it, then you increase your chances of getting the right answer even if you have to guess. Try dissecting difficult words. Notice prefixes and suffixes and words like *may, can, often, rarely*, etc. An answer choice may be wrong because it doesn't contain these words but has words like *exactly* and *never*, which leaves no room for exception.

SWITCHBACK WORDS

Be careful with switchback words such as *but, although*, and *nevertheless*. They will alter the nature of the question and are there to throw you off. Negative words, such as *not* or *except* will subtly reverse the meaning of a question. This trap can easily lead you astray if you are not paying attention to each word in the question. For example, missing the reversal word in the question "Which of the following is not…?," will cause you to answer incorrectly. You might be so confident that you will not reread the question and move on without realizing the original error. A good strategy is to underline or highlight each switchback and negative word in the question to keep track of them easily. Pay close attention to each and every word to avoid this trick.

PRACTICE TESTS

TAKING THE PRACTICE TEST

The practice tests will help you the most if you take them under conditions as close as possible to those of the actual test.

- **Set aside 1 hour of uninterrupted time.**
  That way you can complete the entire test in one sitting.

- **Sit at a desk or table cleared of any other papers, books, and electronic devices.**
  You won't be able to take a dictionary, books, notes, scratch paper, phone, or laptop into the test room.

- **Record your answers on paper, then score your test.**
  Use the answer sheet when completing a practice test to simulate the real testing environment. After completing the practice test, you can score the test yourself.
  Note: The passing grade is 70%, meaning you must get at least 28 answers correct!

PRACTICE TEST 1: ANSWER SHEET

1. Ⓐ Ⓑ Ⓒ Ⓓ 11. Ⓐ Ⓑ Ⓒ Ⓓ 21. Ⓐ Ⓑ Ⓒ Ⓓ 31. Ⓐ Ⓑ Ⓒ Ⓓ

2. Ⓐ Ⓑ Ⓒ Ⓓ 12. Ⓐ Ⓑ Ⓒ Ⓓ 22. Ⓐ Ⓑ Ⓒ Ⓓ 32. Ⓐ Ⓑ Ⓒ Ⓓ

3. Ⓐ Ⓑ Ⓒ Ⓓ 13. Ⓐ Ⓑ Ⓒ Ⓓ 23. Ⓐ Ⓑ Ⓒ Ⓓ 33. Ⓐ Ⓑ Ⓒ Ⓓ

4. Ⓐ Ⓑ Ⓒ Ⓓ 14. Ⓐ Ⓑ Ⓒ Ⓓ 24. Ⓐ Ⓑ Ⓒ Ⓓ 34. Ⓐ Ⓑ Ⓒ Ⓓ

5. Ⓐ Ⓑ Ⓒ Ⓓ 15. Ⓐ Ⓑ Ⓒ Ⓓ 25. Ⓐ Ⓑ Ⓒ Ⓓ 35. Ⓐ Ⓑ Ⓒ Ⓓ

6. Ⓐ Ⓑ Ⓒ Ⓓ 16. Ⓐ Ⓑ Ⓒ Ⓓ 26. Ⓐ Ⓑ Ⓒ Ⓓ 36. Ⓐ Ⓑ Ⓒ Ⓓ

7. Ⓐ Ⓑ Ⓒ Ⓓ 17. Ⓐ Ⓑ Ⓒ Ⓓ 27. Ⓐ Ⓑ Ⓒ Ⓓ 37. Ⓐ Ⓑ Ⓒ Ⓓ

8. Ⓐ Ⓑ Ⓒ Ⓓ 18. Ⓐ Ⓑ Ⓒ Ⓓ 28. Ⓐ Ⓑ Ⓒ Ⓓ 38. Ⓐ Ⓑ Ⓒ Ⓓ

9. Ⓐ Ⓑ Ⓒ Ⓓ 19. Ⓐ Ⓑ Ⓒ Ⓓ 29. Ⓐ Ⓑ Ⓒ Ⓓ 39. Ⓐ Ⓑ Ⓒ Ⓓ

10. Ⓐ Ⓑ Ⓒ Ⓓ 20. Ⓐ Ⓑ Ⓒ Ⓓ 30. Ⓐ Ⓑ Ⓒ Ⓓ 40. Ⓐ Ⓑ Ⓒ Ⓓ

PRACTICE TEST 1

1. What is the consequence of a notary public taking acknowledgments or affidavits without the personal appearance of the individual?

   A. It is considered a felony
   B. It is considered a misdemeanor
   C. It is viewed as a serious offense
   D. It has no consequences

2. Which of the following two statements are correct? A notary public may:

   1. Solemnize a marriage
   2. Take the acknowledgment of parties and witnesses to a written contract of marriage

   A. Only 1
   B. Only 2
   C. 1 and 2
   D. None

3. When a bank's safe deposit box is opened in front of a notary public, the notary shall file with the lessor a certificate under seal which contains:

   1. The date of the opening of the safe deposit box
   2. The name of the lessee
   3. A list (inventory) of the contents

   A. 1 only
   B. 1 and 2 only
   C. 1, 2, and 3
   D. 3 only

4. What ensures that a principal's appearance through communication technology is legitimate for electronic notarization?

   A. The principal's verbal confirmation alone
   B. A valid government-issued ID shown on camera
   C. The notary's personal knowledge or identity verification processes
   D. The principal's physical presence in a pre-approved location

5. Which of the following may a notary public that is duly licensed as an attorney and counselor at law in New York State substitute the words "Notary Public" for?

   A. "Attorney at Law"
   B. "Attorney and Counselor at Law"
   C. "Lawyer"
   D. "Notary Public Lawyer"

6. What is the document used as testimony in a court proceeding?

   A. Instrument
   B. Testament
   C. Deposition
   D. Subpoena

7. Which of the following convictions will bar a candidate to be appointed as a notary public?

   A. Drunken driving
   B. Misdemeanor
   C. A crime
   D. Traffic offenses

8. The following form is used in which clause?
   "Sworn to before me this _____ day of _____"

   A. Pro Se
   B. The Oath
   C. The Affirmation
   D. Jurat

9. What ensures that a principal's appearance through communication technology is legitimate for electronic notarization?

   A. The principal's verbal confirmation alone
   B. A valid government-issued ID shown on camera
   C. The notary's personal knowledge or identity verification processes
   D. The principal's physical presence in a pre-approved location

10. What is a written instrument given to pass title of personal property from vender to vendee?

    A. Affirmation
    B. Bill of Sale
    C. Chattel Paper
    D. Codicil

11. Which of the following people can hold the office of notary public?

    A. A County Sheriff
    B. A former Commissioner of Deeds for NYC who was removed from office
    C. A & B above
    D. None of the above

12. Before performing electronic notarial acts, what must a notary public do?

    A. Take an oath of office in person
    B. Obtain a law degree
    C. Pass a technology exam
    D. Register with the Secretary of State

13. Any person who is not a notary public but who represents himself as such is guilty of:

    A. A misdemeanor
    B. A felony
    C. Harassment
    D. Perjury

14. Which of the following is not true when the Secretary of State issues a duplicate notary public identification card?

    A. The word "duplicate" will stamped across the duplicate identification card
    B. Have the same identification number as the original identification card
    C. Be the exact copy as the original identification card
    D. Fee of $10 will be charged for the duplicate identification card

15. What happens if an electronic notary changes their email address?

    A. Nothing, it's not important
    B. Must notify the Secretary of State within five days

C. Only update their website
D. Send a letter to all clients

16. What is the maximum length of term as a notary public?

    A. 6 months
    B. 1 year
    C. 2 years
    D. 4 years

17. Which of the following acts may a notary public not do on a Sunday?

    A. Take an acknowledgment
    B. Administer an oath
    C. Take an affidavit
    D. Take a deposition

18. What is it called to witness the execution of a written instrument, at the request of the person who makes it, and subscribe the same as a witness?

    A. Endorse
    B. Attest
    C. Certifies
    D. Affirms

19. What role does a "Credential service provider" play in electronic notarization?

    A. Provides notarial seals
    B. Offers legal advice
    C. Trains notaries on law
    D. Issues electronic credentials for identity verification

20. Which of the follow are not defects that will cause a notary public act to be deemed invalid?

    A. The action occurred on a Sunday
    B. The action was outside the jurisdiction of the notary
    C. Misspelling of his name
    D. Expiration of his term

21. What is a misdemeanor?

    A. Intentionally wrongful or improper act
    B. Any crime other than a felony
    C. Unlawful performance of an act
    D. Minor felony

22. Which of the following is not printed on a notary public identification card?

    A. Appointee's name
    B. Address and county
    C. Issued date
    D. Commission term

23. Credential analysis utilizes what to verify an ID's authenticity?

    A. Manual inspection by the notary
    B. Public or private data sources
    C. Central notary database
    D. Only government databases

24. Which class felony is forgery in the second degree?

    A. B
    B. C
    C. D
    D. E

25. What is an executor?

A. A document that verifies the authority of a notary public
B. The placing of an instrument in the hands of a person as a depository
C. The one named in the will to carry out the requirements of a will
D. An instrument that modifies an already existing will

26. What must an electronic notary do if there is a change in their information?

    A. Notify the local notary association
    B. Publish a notice in a local newspaper
    C. Update the information prior to any electronic notarial act
    D. Nothing, changes do not affect notarization

27. What will a notary public who knowingly makes a false certificate be prosecuted for?

    A. Forgery
    B. Misconduct
    C. A misdemeanor
    D. Malpractice

28. What does a county clerk's certificate authenticate?

    A. Authority of a notary public
    B. Authority of a county clerk
    C. Authority of the Secretary of State
    D. None of the above

29. The notary certificate of a witness to the execution of a real estate conveyance is called:

    A. Qualified resident
    B. Official Character
    C. Certificate of acknowledgment
    D. None of the above

30. What must be included in the electronic notarization certificate?

    A. Only the date of the notarization
    B. The notary's physical address
    C. Statement that the act was done using communication technology
    D. The notary's registration number

31. When are conveyances of real property not be recorded?

    A. The conveyance is in a foreign language with no translations
    B. The fee of $5 is not paid before the conveyance
    C. The notary public has taken an acknowledgment from both parties prior
    D. None the above

32. What is the geographical place called where a notary public takes an affidavit or acknowledgment?

    A. State
    B. Town
    C. Locale
    D. Venue

33. What makes an electronic signature reliable for notarial acts?

    A. Unique to the notary and capable of independent verification
    B. Being widely recognized

NEW YORK NOTARY PUBLIC STUDY GUIDE | 93

C. Being created in a secure environment
D. Using the latest technology

34. If the rental fee of a safe deposit box is not paid, the contents in the box can be removed within at least how many days?

   A. 10 days
   B. 30 days
   C. 60 days
   D. 90 days

35. Which of the following statements is not correct? A notary public is:

   A. Authorized to administer oaths
   B. Authorized to administer an oath to himself
   C. Not authorized to administer oaths and affirmations
   D. Authorized to receive and certify acknowledgments

36. What is a chattel?

   A. A security agreement
   B. Personal property such as household goods or fixtures
   C. The Latin word for Jurat
   D. The damages paid for wrongful Notary Public Fees

37. What minimum standard must identity proofing meet for notarization?

   A. Identity Assurance Level
   B. Identity Assurance Level 2
   C. Basic email verification
   D. Social Security number confirmation

38. What is the rule that authorizes a deposition to be taken before a notary public in a civil proceeding?

   A. Criminal Procedure Law
   B. NYS Administrative Code
   C. Family Court Act
   D. Civil Practice Law and Rules

39. A notary public is BEST described as a(n):

   A. Public official
   B. Public officer
   C. Legal counsel
   D. Actuary

40. What does "Communication technology" enable for electronic notarization?

   A. Only audio communication
   B. Simultaneous sight and sound communication
   C. Text-only communication
   D. Email exchanges only

PRACTICE TEST 1: ANSWER KEY

1. C. It is viewed as a serious offense
   Professional Conduct .... Page 1
2. D. None
   Section 11 – Domestic Relations Law .... Page 45
3. C. 1, 2, and 3
   Section 335 – Banking Law .... Page 44
4. C. The notary's personal knowledge or identity verification processes
   Section 182.5 – Satisfactory Evidence of Identity .... Page 66
5. B. "Attorney and Counselor at Law"
   Section 137 – Statement as to authority of notaries public .... Page 28
6. C. Deposition
   Deposition .... Page 79
7. C. A crime
   Section 130 – Appointment of Notaries Public .... Page 5
8. D. Jurat
   Jurat .... Page 80
9. C. The notary's personal knowledge or identity verification processes
   Section 182.5 – Satisfactory Evidence of Identity .... Page 66
10. B. Bill of Sale
    Bill of Sale .... Page 78
11. D. None of the above
    Member of Legislature .... Page 13
    Section 140 – Executive Law .... Page 11
12. D. Register with the Secretary of State
    Section 182.2 – Definitions .... Page 59
13. A. A misdemeanor
    Public Officers Laws .... Page 51
14. C. Be the exact copy as the original identification card
    Section 131 – Procedure of appointment; fees and commissions .... Page 7
15. B. Must notify the Secretary of State within five days
    Section 135-c – Electronic Notarization .... Page 21
16. D. 4 years
    Section 130 – Appointment of Notaries Public .... Page 5
17. D. Take a deposition
    Sunday .... Page 83
18. B. Attest
    Attest .... Page 78
19. D. Issues electronic credentials for identity verification

NEW YORK NOTARY PUBLIC STUDY GUIDE

Section 182.2 – Definitions .... Page 59
20. A. The action occurred on a Sunday
    Section 142-a – Validity of acts of notaries public .... Page 31
21. B. Any crime other than a felony
    Misdemeanor .... Page 81
22. C. Issued date
    Section 131 – Procedure of appointment; fees and commissions .... Page 7
23. B. Public or private data sources
    Section 182.6 – Credential Analysis .... Page 67
24. C. D
    Section 170.10 – Forgery in the second degree .... Page 54
    Section 195.00 – Official misconduct .... Page 56
25. C. The one named in the will to carry out the provisions of a will
    Executor .... Page 80
26. C. Update the information prior to any electronic notarial act
    Section 182.4 – Additional Requirements for Electronic Notaries .... Page 64
27. A. Forgery
    Section 170.10 – Forgery in the second degree .... Page 54
28. A. Authority of a notary public
    Authentication (Notarial) .... Page 78
29. C. Certificate of acknowledgment
    Section 306 – Certificate of acknowledgment or proof .... Page 37
30. C. Statement that the act was done using communication technology
    Section 135-c – Electronic Notarization .... Page 21
31. A. The conveyance is in a foreign language with no translations
    Section 333 – When conveyances of real property not to be recorded .... Page 43
32. D. Venue
    Venue .... Page 83
33. A. Unique to the notary and capable of independent verification
    Section 182.4 – Additional Requirements for Electronic Notaries .... Page 64
34. B. 30 days
    Section 335 – Banking Law .... Page 44
35. C. Not authorized to administer oaths and affirmations
    Section 135 – Powers and duties .... Page 17
36. B. Personal property such as household goods or fixtures
    Chattel .... Page 78
37. B. Identity Assurance Level 2
    Section 182.7 – Identity Proofing .... Page 69
38. D. Civil Practice Law and Rules
    Rule 3113 – Civil Practice Law and Rules .... Page 45
39. B. Public officer

Public Officers Laws .... Page 51
40. B. Simultaneous sight and sound communication
Section 135-c – Electronic Notarization .... Page 21

PRACTICE TEST 2: ANSWER SHEET

1. Ⓐ Ⓑ Ⓒ Ⓓ   11. Ⓐ Ⓑ Ⓒ Ⓓ   21. Ⓐ Ⓑ Ⓒ Ⓓ   31. Ⓐ Ⓑ Ⓒ Ⓓ

2. Ⓐ Ⓑ Ⓒ Ⓓ   12. Ⓐ Ⓑ Ⓒ Ⓓ   22. Ⓐ Ⓑ Ⓒ Ⓓ   32. Ⓐ Ⓑ Ⓒ Ⓓ

3. Ⓐ Ⓑ Ⓒ Ⓓ   13. Ⓐ Ⓑ Ⓒ Ⓓ   23. Ⓐ Ⓑ Ⓒ Ⓓ   33. Ⓐ Ⓑ Ⓒ Ⓓ

4. Ⓐ Ⓑ Ⓒ Ⓓ   14. Ⓐ Ⓑ Ⓒ Ⓓ   24. Ⓐ Ⓑ Ⓒ Ⓓ   34. Ⓐ Ⓑ Ⓒ Ⓓ

5. Ⓐ Ⓑ Ⓒ Ⓓ   15. Ⓐ Ⓑ Ⓒ Ⓓ   25. Ⓐ Ⓑ Ⓒ Ⓓ   35. Ⓐ Ⓑ Ⓒ Ⓓ

6. Ⓐ Ⓑ Ⓒ Ⓓ   16. Ⓐ Ⓑ Ⓒ Ⓓ   26. Ⓐ Ⓑ Ⓒ Ⓓ   36. Ⓐ Ⓑ Ⓒ Ⓓ

7. Ⓐ Ⓑ Ⓒ Ⓓ   17. Ⓐ Ⓑ Ⓒ Ⓓ   27. Ⓐ Ⓑ Ⓒ Ⓓ   37. Ⓐ Ⓑ Ⓒ Ⓓ

8. Ⓐ Ⓑ Ⓒ Ⓓ   18. Ⓐ Ⓑ Ⓒ Ⓓ   28. Ⓐ Ⓑ Ⓒ Ⓓ   38. Ⓐ Ⓑ Ⓒ Ⓓ

9. Ⓐ Ⓑ Ⓒ Ⓓ   19. Ⓐ Ⓑ Ⓒ Ⓓ   29. Ⓐ Ⓑ Ⓒ Ⓓ   39. Ⓐ Ⓑ Ⓒ Ⓓ

10. Ⓐ Ⓑ Ⓒ Ⓓ   20. Ⓐ Ⓑ Ⓒ Ⓓ   30. Ⓐ Ⓑ Ⓒ Ⓓ   40. Ⓐ Ⓑ Ⓒ Ⓓ

PRACTICE TEST 2

1. What constitutes satisfactory evidence of identity for electronic notarization?

    A. Only a government-issued ID card
    B. A digital handshake
    C. Identity verification, credential analysis, and identity proofing
    D. A username and password

2. Which of the following acts can be performed by a notary public on Sunday?

    A. Certified original certificate of government doc photocopy
    B. Affidavit
    C. Someone's signature to their own will by non-attorney notary
    D. A contract of marriage

3. Under what condition can a notary refuse to perform a notarial act?

    A. If the principal offers payment
    B. If the notary is busy at the time requested
    C. If the notary is not satisfied with the principal's competence or voluntariness
    D. If the notary does not like the document's content

4. Who has some limited rights to practice law as a non-attorney?

    A. Law students after 2 semesters and have not failed bar exam 2 times
    B. Officers for the prevention of cruelty
    C. Law school graduates
    D. All the above

5. A notary public may not be removed from office for misconduct unless the person:

    1. is served with a copy of the charges against him or her
    2. has had an opportunity to be heard

    A. 1 and 2 are not correct
    B. Only 1 is correct
    C. Only 2 is correct
    D. 1 and 2 are correct

6. What disqualifies a notary public from reappointment?

    A. Failing to comply with any part requirements related to notarial acts
    B. Not using electronic notarization
    C. Moving out of state
    D. Not renewing on time

7. What is it called when a notary public declares the following statement on an affidavit?

    "Sworn to before me this _____ day of _____, 20_____"

    A. Codicil
    B. Contract
    C. Jurat
    D. Lien

8. What is the total commission fee for the appointment of a notary public?

   A. $10
   B. $20
   C. $60
   D. None of the above

9. Can notaries use third-party services for record storage?

   A. Yes, if secured with a password or other authentication
   B. No, all records must be kept physically by the notary
   C. Only for electronic notarial acts
   D. Yes, without any security measures

10. What is "laches"?

    A. A device to lock a notary logbook safely away from the public
    B. The act of carrying on a lawsuit.
    C. The delay or negligence in asserting one's rights in court
    D. None of the above

11. How are applications and registrations for notary public submitted?

    A. Via email to the secretary of state
    B. In person only
    C. Through the department of state's division of licensing as prescribed
    D. On any website

12. What is required of the communication technology used for electronic notarial acts?

    A. Only audio clarity
    B. High-definition video only
    C. Sufficient audio and visual clarity for live interaction
    D. Email confirmation capability

13. Which scenario does not disqualify a notary public from performing notary duties?

    A. A notary public who is a grantee in a conveyance
    B. A notary public who is a mortgagor in a conveyance
    C. A notary public beneficially interested in a conveyance
    D. None of the above

14. What is every instrument in writing, except a will, that transfers real estate interests?

    A. Conveyance
    B. Escrow
    C. Vendor receipt
    D. Duress

15. What is the fee for electronic notarial acts?

    A. $10 per act
    B. $25 per act
    C. Free
    D. Variable, set by the notary

16. What is an instrument that is put into the custody of a third-party to be held until the occurrence of an event?

    A. Lien
    B. Mortgage on real property
    C. Escrow

D. Trust

17. Which of the following is a legal right attached to a specific property until a debt is paid?

    A. Lien
    B. Mortgage on real property
    C. Laches
    D. Contract

18. For electronic notarization, when is a third-party identity proofing required?

    A. When the individual is personally known to the notary
    B. Always, regardless of personal acquaintance
    C. Only if the individual appears remotely and is not known to the notary
    D. Never, electronic notaries do not require identity proofing

19. What is a crime that is not a felony?

    A. Regulatory offence
    B. Misdemeanor
    C. Protest
    D. Duress

20. Which of the following acts can a notary public do if he is a shareholder and has financial interest in a corporation?

    A. Protest for non-payment
    B. Administer an oath to a party of the corporation
    C. Take the acknowledgment of the CEO of the corporation
    D. None of the above

21. What information must be included in the notarial records?

    A. Date, time, type of notarial acts, and principal's credit score
    B. Date, time, type of notarial acts, and identification details of individuals
    C. Notary's personal diary entries
    D. Only the names of individuals notarized

22. If a notary public refuses to notarize an affidavit after all requirements are met, what is the potential maximum sentence of imprisonment?

    A. 1 month
    B. 3 months
    C. 6 months
    D. 1 year

23. Who can issue certified copies of a public record?

    A. A notary public
    B. An attorney at law
    C. A public official who holds custody of the original
    D. None of the above

24. What activities are prohibited for a notary public because they are considered practicing law?

    A. Drawing legal papers like wills and contracts
    B. Offering notary services
    C. Notarizing documents within their legal rights
    D. Witnessing a signature

25. Can a member of the New York legislature be appointed to a paid civil office?

    A. Yes, without any conditions
    B. Yes, if it's a part-time position
    C. No, unless they resign
    D. Only to unpaid positions

26. Which of the following is in the requirements to become a Notary Public in New York?

    A. Be at least 18 years old
    B. No special education or common school level
    C. Be a resident of NYS
    D. All the above

27. How soon must a notary notify the secretary of state after a change of name, address, or email?

    A. Within 30 days
    B. Within 10 business days
    C. Within 5 days
    D. Immediately

28. What does notary public subject himself to by asking or receiving more than the statutory allowance for administering an oath in connection with an affidavit?

    1. Possible removal from office
    2. Criminal prosecution
    3. Civil lawsuit

    A. 3 only
    B. 1 and 3 only
    C. 1, 2, and 3
    D. 2 only

29. A sentence of imprisonment for a Class A misdemeanor will be imposed by the court and not exceed:

    A. 3 months
    B. 1 year
    C. 2 years
    D. 4 years

30. What is required for a notary to validate the identity of any principal?

    A. A written testimonial from a third party
    B. Satisfactory evidence of identity
    C. A social media background check
    D. Verification via a phone call

31. What can happen to a notary public taking acknowledgment of a conveyance who is guilty of malfeasance?

    A. May be removed from office
    B. Liable to treble damages
    C. Guilty of a misdemeanor
    D. Liable in damages to the person injured

32. What does the "Electronic signature" require?

    A. Ink signature scanned
    B. Compliance with state technology law
    C. Witness signature
    D. Any digital mark

33. What is a notary public guilty of if he makes a statement he knows to be false under oath?

    A. Malpractice
    B. Perjury
    C. Contempt of court
    D. Misdemeanor

34. Where must a notary be located to perform electronic notarial acts in New York?

    A. Within the United States
    B. Anywhere, as long as they are online
    C. Within New York State boundaries
    D. In a government office

35. Which of the following cases can the supreme court punish anyone for criminal contempt?

    A. Practices law unlawfully
    B. Refuses to notarize an affidavit
    C. Performs any duties of a notary before becoming a notary public
    D. Advertises to the public that he is a notary public

36. A person who starts a civil lawsuit is called the:

    A. Appellant
    B. Defendant
    C. Plaintiff
    D. Antagonist

37. What must an "Electronic signature" used by an electronic notary comply with?

    A. State Technology Law and additional part requirements
    B. The notary's personal preference
    C. Federal signature guidelines
    D. The principal's request

38. What is the fee to administer an oath or affirmation?

    A. 75 cents
    B. $1
    C. $2
    D. $5

39. What must a notary include on each instrument requiring an oath or affirmation?

    A. Their personal contact information
    B. The principal's date of birth
    C. The notary public's official number
    D. A unique document identification number

40. How must a notary be able to interact with identification cards during electronic notarization?

    A. View and capture both sides digitally
    B. Physically hold the card
    C. Ask the principal to describe the card
    D. Use a third-party verification service

PRACTICE TEST 2: ANSWER KEY

1. C. Identity verification, credential analysis, and identity proofing
   Section 182.5 – Satisfactory Evidence of Identity .... Page 66
2. B. Affidavit
   Sunday .... Page 83
3. C. If the notary is not satisfied with the principal's competence or voluntariness
   Section 135-c – Electronic Notarization .... Page 21
4. D. All the above
   Section 130 – Appointment of Notaries Public .... Page 5
5. D. 1 and 2 are correct
   Section 137 – Statement as to authority of notaries public .... Page 29
6. A. Failing to comply with any part requirements related to notarial acts
   Section 182.10 – Applications, Registrations and Renewals .... Page 72
7. C. Jurat
   Jurat .... Page 80
8. C. $60
   Section 131 – Procedure of appointment; fees and commissions .... Page 7
9. A. Yes, if secured with a password or other authentication
   Section 182.9 – Recordkeeping and Reporting .... Page 71
10. C. The delay or negligence in asserting one's rights in court
    Laches .... Page 80
11. C. Through the department of state's division of licensing as prescribed
    Section 182.10 – Applications, Registrations and Renewals .... Page 72
12. C. Sufficient audio and visual clarity for live interaction
    Section 182.8 – Communication Technology .... Page 70
13. D. None of the above
    Notary public - disqualifications .... Page 14
14. A. Conveyance
    Conveyance .... Page 79
15. B. $25 per act
    Section 182.11 – Fees .... Page 74
16. C. Escrow
    Escrow .... Page 79
17. A. Lien
    Lien .... Page 80
18. C. Only if the individual appears remotely and is not known to the notary
    Section 182.5 – Satisfactory Evidence of Identity .... Page 66
19. B. Misdemeanor
    Misdemeanor .... Page 81
20. A. Protest for non-payment

104 | NEW YORK NOTARY PUBLIC STUDY GUIDE

Section 135 – Powers and duties .... Page 17
21. B. Date, time, type of notarial acts, and identification details of individuals
    Section 182.9 – Recordkeeping and Reporting .... Page 71
22. D. 1 year
    Section 70.15 – Sentences of imprisonment .... Page 54
23. C. A public official who holds custody of the original
    Certified Copy .... Page 78
24. A. Drawing legal papers like wills and contracts
    Professional Conduct .... Page 1
25. D. Only to unpaid positions
    Member of Legislature .... Page 14
26. D. All the above
    Section 130 – Appointment of Notaries Public .... Page 5
27. C. Within 5 days
    Section 182.3 – Requirements for Notaries .... Page 62
28. C. 1, 2, and 3
    Section 67 – Fees of public officers .... Page 51
29. B. 1 year
    Section 70.15 – Sentences of imprisonment .... Page 54
30. B. Satisfactory evidence of identity
    Section 182.3 – Requirements for Notaries .... Page 62
31. D. Liable in damages to the person injured
    Section 330 – Officers guilty of malfeasance liable for damages .... Page 42
32. B. Compliance with state technology law
    Section 135-c – Electronic Notarization .... Page 21
33. B. Perjury
    Perjury .... Page 57
34. C. Within New York State boundaries
    Section 182.4 – Additional Requirements for Electronic Notaries .... Page 64
35. A. Practices law unlawfully
    Section 750 – Power of courts to punish for criminal contempts .... Page 50
36. C. Plaintiff
    Plaintiff .... Page 81
37. A. State Technology Law and additional part requirements
    Section 182.2 – Definitions .... Page 59
38. C. $2
    Section 136 – Notarial fees .... Page 28
39. C. The notary public's official number
    Section 182.8 – Communication Technology .... Page 70
40. A. View and capture both sides digitally
    Section 182.3 – Requirements for Notaries .... Page 62

NEW YORK NOTARY PUBLIC STUDY GUIDE | 105

PRACTICE TEST 3: ANSWER SHEET

1. Ⓐ Ⓑ Ⓒ Ⓓ   11. Ⓐ Ⓑ Ⓒ Ⓓ   21. Ⓐ Ⓑ Ⓒ Ⓓ   31. Ⓐ Ⓑ Ⓒ Ⓓ

2. Ⓐ Ⓑ Ⓒ Ⓓ   12. Ⓐ Ⓑ Ⓒ Ⓓ   22. Ⓐ Ⓑ Ⓒ Ⓓ   32. Ⓐ Ⓑ Ⓒ Ⓓ

3. Ⓐ Ⓑ Ⓒ Ⓓ   13. Ⓐ Ⓑ Ⓒ Ⓓ   23. Ⓐ Ⓑ Ⓒ Ⓓ   33. Ⓐ Ⓑ Ⓒ Ⓓ

4. Ⓐ Ⓑ Ⓒ Ⓓ   14. Ⓐ Ⓑ Ⓒ Ⓓ   24. Ⓐ Ⓑ Ⓒ Ⓓ   34. Ⓐ Ⓑ Ⓒ Ⓓ

5. Ⓐ Ⓑ Ⓒ Ⓓ   15. Ⓐ Ⓑ Ⓒ Ⓓ   25. Ⓐ Ⓑ Ⓒ Ⓓ   35. Ⓐ Ⓑ Ⓒ Ⓓ

6. Ⓐ Ⓑ Ⓒ Ⓓ   16. Ⓐ Ⓑ Ⓒ Ⓓ   26. Ⓐ Ⓑ Ⓒ Ⓓ   36. Ⓐ Ⓑ Ⓒ Ⓓ

7. Ⓐ Ⓑ Ⓒ Ⓓ   17. Ⓐ Ⓑ Ⓒ Ⓓ   27. Ⓐ Ⓑ Ⓒ Ⓓ   37. Ⓐ Ⓑ Ⓒ Ⓓ

8. Ⓐ Ⓑ Ⓒ Ⓓ   18. Ⓐ Ⓑ Ⓒ Ⓓ   28. Ⓐ Ⓑ Ⓒ Ⓓ   38. Ⓐ Ⓑ Ⓒ Ⓓ

9. Ⓐ Ⓑ Ⓒ Ⓓ   19. Ⓐ Ⓑ Ⓒ Ⓓ   29. Ⓐ Ⓑ Ⓒ Ⓓ   39. Ⓐ Ⓑ Ⓒ Ⓓ

10. Ⓐ Ⓑ Ⓒ Ⓓ   20. Ⓐ Ⓑ Ⓒ Ⓓ   30. Ⓐ Ⓑ Ⓒ Ⓓ   40. Ⓐ Ⓑ Ⓒ Ⓓ

PRACTICE TEST 3

1. What is the maximum sentence for a class E felony?

    A. 4 years
    B. 7 years
    C. 3 years
    D. There is no limit

2. What security feature is essential for the communication technology used in electronic notarization?

    A. Password protection for the video session
    B. Signal transmission secure from unauthorized interception
    C. Encryption of the notary's signature only
    D. Biometric verification of the principal

3. Which of the following is an ex parte statement?

    A. Deposition
    B. Acknowledgment
    C. Affidavit
    D. Conveyance

4. For what purpose can an electronic notary use their designated electronic signature?

    A. Personal and notarial acts
    B. Only for electronic notarial acts as specified
    C. Signing personal documents
    D. Online verification processes

5. Where can the acknowledgment of a conveyance of real property be made?

    A. Within the district the notary public is authorized to perform official duties
    B. Within the City of New York
    C. Within the county of residence the notary public is commissioned in
    D. All of the above

6. What is the fee for a duplicate notary public identification card?

    A. $5
    B. $10
    C. $15
    D. $50

7. What is it called when a person takes a solemn declaration who conscientiously decline taking an oath?

    A. Affirmation
    B. Attest
    C. Acknowledgment
    D. Affidavit

8. What is an "Electronic record"?

    A. Paper documents only
    B. Handwritten notes
    C. Official government documents
    D. Information stored by electronic means

9. What is a formal declaration before an authorized officer by a person who has

NEW YORK NOTARY PUBLIC STUDY GUIDE | 107

executed an instrument that such execution is his act and deed?

A. Certified Copy
B. Chattel Paper
C. Acknowledgment
D. Conveyance

10. Who can be a "Principal" in the context of notarization?

A. Only New York residents
B. Government officials
C. Only notaries public
D. Individuals whose signatures are notarized

11. What must be stated by the subscribing witness when executing a conveyance?

A. The number of years he has owned the real property
B. The subscribing witness' place of residence
C. The county where the conveyance is executed
D. The venue where the conveyance is executed

12. Where can a New York State notary public administer oaths and take affidavits?

A. United States
B. New York State
C. The county of residence only
D. None of the above

13. What details about the verification procedures must be recorded?

A. The verification method and any witnesses' names
B. The principal's social security number
C. The notary's personal opinions
D. The weather conditions during notarization

14. When is it NOT illegal to take an acknowledgment over the telephone?

A. It is always illegal
B. When the notary public has satisfactory evidence that the person making it is the person described
C. When the notary public is personally acquainted with the person making it
D. When no jurat is required

15. A person appointed by the court to manage the estate of a deceased person who did not leave behind a will is called:

A. An executor
B. A plaintiff
C. An administrator
D. A deponent

16. What security measures must an electronic notary maintain for their electronic signature and seal?

A. Share them with the secretary of state only
B. Keep them under sole control and not disclose unless legally required
C. Use 2-factor authentication
D. Store them on a private cloud

17. What is the fee for taking an acknowledgment and swearing two witnesses?

A. $4
B. $1
C. $6
D. $7.50

18. What is the state law that refers that certain contracts must be in writing so that they can be enforceable at law?

    A. Contract
    B. Statute of frauds
    C. Statute of limitations
    D. Litigation

19. What is prohibited for sheriffs in the State of New York according to the constitution?

    A. Holding any other public office
    B. Running for mayor while serving as sheriff
    C. Receiving compensation from another job
    D. Serving as a notary public

20. What is a notary public guilty of when he issues an instrument knowing that it contains false information with the intent to defraud?

    A. Issuing a false certificate
    B. Official misconduct
    C. Perjury
    D. Duress

21. How much must notaries pay to renew their commission?

    A. $25
    B. $60
    C. $15
    D. $10

22. What can a person take if that person declines to take an oath because of religious reasons?

    A. Codicil
    B. Affirmation
    C. Contract
    D. Lien

23. What is the role of the National Institute of Standards and Technology (NIST) in identity proofing?

    A. Provides the physical location for notary registration
    B. Outlines the minimum standard for identity proofing
    C. Directly conducts identity proofing for notaries
    D. Issues notary public licenses

24. What is a notary public guilty of when he refuses to officiate on request?

    A. Forgery
    B. Perjury
    C. A felony
    D. A misdemeanor

25. What is it called when something that has value and is given to induce someone to enter into a contract?

    A. Consideration
    B. Will
    C. Chattel
    D. Real property

NEW YORK NOTARY PUBLIC STUDY GUIDE

26. Which of the following instruments can a notary public who is not a lawyer prepare?

    A. A will or codicil
    B. A deed or an assignment
    C. A mortgage
    D. None of the above

27. What qualifies as an "Electronic notarial act"?

    A. Signing a document with a pen
    B. An act done in person without technology
    C. Using communication technology for notarial acts
    D. Email verification

28. Which of the following is a certificate of proof or acknowledgment or oath signed by a notary public?

    A. Authentication
    B. Affirmation
    C. Chattel Paper
    D. Will

29. What is the application fee for a notary public commission?

    A. $25
    B. $60
    C. $15
    D. $10

30. What is the formal statement by a notary public declaring a default in payment on a promissory note?

    A. Affidavit
    B. Jurat
    C. Protest
    D. Proof

31. What must be verified when an electronic notary public applies for reappointment?

    A. Their identity and residence
    B. Accuracy of all information on file and compliance with all requirements
    C. Number of notarizations performed
    D. Feedback from clients

32. What is a notary public guilty of when he knowingly refrains from performing his duty that is imposed by law?

    A. Official misconduct
    B. Class A misdemeanor
    C. Fraudulent practice
    D. A and B

33. What does the law say about requiring notarial transactions to exclusively use electronic notarization?

    A. No notary or business can exclusively require it
    B. It's mandatory for all notaries
    C. It's encouraged to speed up the process
    D. Only applicable for transactions over $10,000

34. Under what circumstance is the notary permitted to receive a greater fee for a service than normally allowed by law?

    A. When travel expenses are incurred

B. When the affidavits exceed one printed page
C. When personal inconvenience or extenuating circumstances
D. Under no circumstance

35. When must a notary disqualify themselves from performing a notarial act?

    A. When they are performing the act outside of New York State
    B. If they are a party or have a direct interest in the transaction
    C. If the act is requested on a weekend
    D. When the document is in a foreign language

36. What is the act of carrying on a lawsuit?

    A. Civil suit
    B. Litigation
    C. Protestation
    D. Perjury

37. Who can perform an "Electronic notarial act"?

    A. Notaries physically present in New York
    B. Any public official
    C. Only the Secretary of State
    D. Remote witnesses

38. Who is a notary public not allowed to administer an oath to?

    A. The Secretary of State
    B. A military officer
    C. Himself/herself
    D. A member of the legislature

39. What additional records must all notaries public maintain besides video and audio recordings?

    A. Only records of electronic notarial acts
    B. Detailed logs of their personal information
    C. Records documenting compliance with legal requirements
    D. Copies of all documents notarized

40. What is the fee for a protest of non-payment or non-acceptance?

    A. A. 75 cents for the first one and 10 cents for each additional notice of protest
    B. $1 for the first one and 10 cents for each additional notice of protest
    C. $5 for up to 4 notice of protests
    D. $5 for unlimited notice of protests within 1 day

PRACTICE TEST 3: ANSWER KEY

1. A. 4 years
   Section 70.00 – Sentence of imprisonment for felony .... Page 53
2. B. Signal transmission secure from unauthorized interception
   Section 182.8 – Communication Technology .... Page 70
3. C. Affidavit
   Affidavit .... Page 77
4. B. Only for electronic notarial acts as specified
   Section 182.4 – Additional Requirements for Electronic Notaries .... Page 64
5. D. All of the above
   Section 298 – Acknowledgments and proofs within the state .... Page 34
6. B. $10
   Section 131 – Procedure of appointment; fees and commissions .... Page 7
7. A. Affirmation
   Affirmation .... Page 77
8. D. Information stored by electronic means
   Section 135-c – Electronic Notarization .... Page 21
9. C. Acknowledgment
   Acknowledgment .... Page 77
10. D. Individuals whose signatures are notarized
    Section 135-c – Electronic Notarization .... Page 21
11. B. The subscribing witness' place of residence
    Section 304 – Proof by subscribing witness .... Page 36
12. B. New York State
    Section 130 – Appointment of Notaries Public .... Page 5
13. A. The verification method and any witnesses' names
    Section 182.9 – Recordkeeping and Reporting .... Page 71
14. A. It is always illegal
    Acknowledgment .... Page 77
15. C. An administrator
    Administrator .... Page 77
16. B. Keep them under sole control and not disclose unless legally required
    Section 182.4 – Additional Requirements for Electronic Notaries .... Page 64
17. C. $6
    Section 135 – Powers and duties .... Page 17
18. B. Statute of frauds
    Statute of Frauds .... Page 83
19. A. Holding any other public office
    Sheriffs .... Page 14
20. A. Issuing a false certificate

    Section 175.40 – Issuing a false certificate .... Page 55
21. B. $60
    Section 182.11 – Fees .... Page 74
22. B. Affirmation
    Affirmation .... Page 77
23. B. Outlines the minimum standard for identity proofing
    Section 182.7 – Identity Proofing .... Page 69
24. D. A misdemeanor
    Notary must officiate on request .... Page 57
25. A. Consideration
    Consideration .... Page 79
26. D. None of the above
    Section 484 – None but attorneys to practice in the state .... Page 48
27. C. Using communication technology for notarial acts
    Section 135-c – Electronic Notarization .... Page 21
28. A. Authentication
    Authentication (Notarial) .... Page 78
29. B. $60
    Section 182.11 – Fees .... Page 74
30. C. Protest
    Protest .... Page 82
31. B. Accuracy of all information on file and compliance with all requirements
    Section 182.10 – Applications, Registrations and Renewals .... Page 72
32. D. A and B
    Section 195.00 – Official misconduct .... Page 56
33. A. No notary or business can exclusively require it
    Section 135-c – Electronic Notarization .... Page 21
34. D. Under no circumstance
    Section 67 – Fees of public officers .... Page 51
35. B. If they are a party or have a direct interest in the transaction
    Notary public - disqualifications .... Page 14
36. B. Litigation
    Litigation .... Page 81
37. A. Notaries physically present in New York
    Section 135-c – Electronic Notarization .... Page 21
38. C. Himself/herself
    Oath .... Page 81
39. C. Records documenting compliance with legal requirements
    Section 182.9 – Recordkeeping and Reporting .... Page 71
40. A. 75 cents for the first one and 10 cents for each additional notice of protest
    Section 135 – Powers and duties .... Page 17

PRACTICE TEST 4: ANSWER SHEET

1. Ⓐ Ⓑ Ⓒ Ⓓ 11. Ⓐ Ⓑ Ⓒ Ⓓ 21. Ⓐ Ⓑ Ⓒ Ⓓ 31. Ⓐ Ⓑ Ⓒ Ⓓ

2. Ⓐ Ⓑ Ⓒ Ⓓ 12. Ⓐ Ⓑ Ⓒ Ⓓ 22. Ⓐ Ⓑ Ⓒ Ⓓ 32. Ⓐ Ⓑ Ⓒ Ⓓ

3. Ⓐ Ⓑ Ⓒ Ⓓ 13. Ⓐ Ⓑ Ⓒ Ⓓ 23. Ⓐ Ⓑ Ⓒ Ⓓ 33. Ⓐ Ⓑ Ⓒ Ⓓ

4. Ⓐ Ⓑ Ⓒ Ⓓ 14. Ⓐ Ⓑ Ⓒ Ⓓ 24. Ⓐ Ⓑ Ⓒ Ⓓ 34. Ⓐ Ⓑ Ⓒ Ⓓ

5. Ⓐ Ⓑ Ⓒ Ⓓ 15. Ⓐ Ⓑ Ⓒ Ⓓ 25. Ⓐ Ⓑ Ⓒ Ⓓ 35. Ⓐ Ⓑ Ⓒ Ⓓ

6. Ⓐ Ⓑ Ⓒ Ⓓ 16. Ⓐ Ⓑ Ⓒ Ⓓ 26. Ⓐ Ⓑ Ⓒ Ⓓ 36. Ⓐ Ⓑ Ⓒ Ⓓ

7. Ⓐ Ⓑ Ⓒ Ⓓ 17. Ⓐ Ⓑ Ⓒ Ⓓ 27. Ⓐ Ⓑ Ⓒ Ⓓ 37. Ⓐ Ⓑ Ⓒ Ⓓ

8. Ⓐ Ⓑ Ⓒ Ⓓ 18. Ⓐ Ⓑ Ⓒ Ⓓ 28. Ⓐ Ⓑ Ⓒ Ⓓ 38. Ⓐ Ⓑ Ⓒ Ⓓ

9. Ⓐ Ⓑ Ⓒ Ⓓ 19. Ⓐ Ⓑ Ⓒ Ⓓ 29. Ⓐ Ⓑ Ⓒ Ⓓ 39. Ⓐ Ⓑ Ⓒ Ⓓ

10. Ⓐ Ⓑ Ⓒ Ⓓ 20. Ⓐ Ⓑ Ⓒ Ⓓ 30. Ⓐ Ⓑ Ⓒ Ⓓ 40. Ⓐ Ⓑ Ⓒ Ⓓ

PRACTICE TEST 4

1. What is the educational requirement for a notary public?

   A. Common school education
   B. High school diploma
   C. College degree
   D. None

2. What is the primary purpose of credential analysis in online notarization?

   A. To collect personal data
   B. To confirm the validity of an identification credential
   C. To increase service fees
   D. To create a database of users

3. What is the fee for a county clerk's certificate of official character?

   A. $25
   B. $50
   C. $1
   D. $5

4. Which of the following is required to be a notary public?

   A. Be a United States citizen
   B. Be a resident of the state
   C. Have a place of business in the state
   D. Be a registered voter

5. What is the fee charged to a person for an affidavit at the county clerk's office?

   A. $2
   B. $2 for each original signature witnessed
   C. .75 (cents) for the first one and .10 (cents) for the second one
   D. Notary services are free during normal business hours

6. What is "Credential analysis" used for in electronic notarization?

   A. Determining the cost of services
   B. Verifying the identity of individuals
   C. Analyzing digital signatures
   D. Assessing the notary's qualifications

7. At what age must a notary public be at time of application for appointment?

   A. 18
   B. 20
   C. 21
   D. 25

8. Which of the following must a person do to continue to be a notary public in NYS if he moves out of the state and does not maintain an office in NYS?

   A. Pay an additional $15 out of state fee
   B. Become a notary public in the other state
   C. Get NY driver's license
   D. None of the above

9. What do the witnesses to a will sign?

   A. The certificate of acknowledgment
   B. Attestation clause
   C. Identity verification form
   D. The affidavit

10. How must electronic notaries secure the signal transmission?

    A. Secure from interception
    B. Open to all for transparency
    C. Through public Wi-Fi
    D. Via unencrypted email

11. What is the fee for the certification of a notarial signature by a county clerk?

    A. $0.50
    B. $0.75
    C. $1
    D. $3

12. Which of the following is the clause, located at the end of a will, where the witnesses certify that the instrument has been executed before them?

    A. Attestation clause
    B. Clause of will
    C. Subordination clause
    D. None of the above

13. Who approves the appointment of a notary public?

    A. An attorney at law from NYS
    B. County Clerk
    C. Secretary of State
    D. Town judge where the Notary resides

14. What is the fee for electronic notarial act registration?

    A. $60
    B. $25
    C. $15
    D. Free of charge

15. What is the following declaration a form of?

    "Do you solemnly, sincerely, and truly, declare and affirm that the statements made by you are true and correct."

    A. Contract
    B. Conveyance
    C. Affirmation
    D. An oath

16. Who is responsible for performing credential analysis for online notarization?

    A. The individual seeking notarization
    B. The online notary public themselves
    C. A third-party service provider approved by the notary
    D. The secretary of state

17. A statement sworn before a notary public personally signed by the affiant is an example of which of the following?

    A. Codicil
    B. Affidavit
    C. Jurat
    D. Oath

18. A person named by a court to administer the estate of a man who has died without leaving a will is called the:

    A. Executor
    B. Intestate
    C. Administrator
    D. Surrogate

19. When can a notary public apply for reappointment?

    A. Anytime during their term
    B. Within 90 days before their commission expires
    C. Only after their commission has expired
    D. After completing additional training

20. Which degree in forgery is a person guilty of when he has the intent to defraud, injure or deceive another?

    A. First
    B. Second
    C. Third
    D. Forth

21. What is an apostile?

    A. An authentication certified for international use
    B. A notary public application
    C. Class D felony
    D. The administrator of a will appointed by the court

22. Who can appoint a member of the legislature as a notary public?

    A. The Governor
    B. The Senate
    C. The Secretary of State
    D. A member of the New York legislature

23. What is a requirement for all parties in a transaction requiring a notarial act?

    A. They must all have a notary license
    B. They must be residents of New York State
    C. Personal appearance for the duration of the transaction
    D. All parties must sign the document beforehand

24. The signature and seal of a county clerk upon a certificate of the official character of a notary public may be:

    A. Printed or photographed
    B. Engraved
    C. A facsimile
    D. All of the above

25. Who is a notary entitled to collect a fee from for administering the oath of office?

    A. Member of the legislature
    B. A military officer
    C. A clerk of the poll
    D. None of the above

26. Is it permissible for a notary public to execute an acknowledgment of the execution of a will?

    A. Yes, in all cases
    B. Only in person
    C. No, it cannot be deemed equivalent to an attestation clause
    D. Yes, if the notary is also a lawyer

27. What is required for satisfactory evidence of identity for in-person notarization?

    A. A verbal confirmation of identity

B. A valid, current ID with photo, physical description, and signature
C. A social media profile check
D. A letter of introduction

28. Which of the following is a notary public guilty of when he takes an acknowledgment over the telephone?

A. Forgery
B. Misdemeanor
C. Felony
D. None of the above

29. What happens when a New York legislator accepts a civil office appointment?

A. They receive a bonus
B. They vacate their seat in the legislature
C. They automatically become governor
D. Nothing changes

30. Which of the following is not eligible for the office of notary public?

A. Commissioner of elections
B. Sheriff
C. Member of the legislature
D. Inspector of elections

31. How can a notary verify the identity of an individual they personally know?

A. By taking their word for it
B. Attestation of personal knowledge
C. Asking for a password
D. A quick online search

32. What is required for an indictment for perjury on an affidavit?

A. Affiant saying "I do" or words of like meaning after the oath is read
B. Affiant nodding head yes
C. Affiant putting thumb print in designated box on form
D. All the above

33. Who can issue the certificate of official character of a notary public?

A. The notary public named in the certificate
B. A notary public who is not named in the certificate
C. Secretary of State
D. Any public official

34. What information is required when registering for electronic notarization?

A. Only the notary's name and email address
B. Name, address, commission details, electronic technology description, and electronic signature exemplar
C. A list of previously notarized documents
D. Recommendations from three clients

35. Which of the following is not an example a misdemeanor?

A. A person found guilty of contempt of court
B. A person removed from office performs an act as a notary public
C. A notary public refuses to notarize an affidavit

D. None of the above

36. Can a notary refuse to perform an electronic notarization?

   A. Never, it's mandatory
   B. Yes, if not satisfied with the principal's competency or signature voluntariness
   C. Only on weekends
   D. If the notary is on vacation

37. What is the writing that indicates that the holder is owed money and has interest in specified goods?

   A. Chattel
   B. Chattel paper
   C. Certificate of acknowledgment
   D. Certificate of official character

38. What does "Personal appearance" entail for notarization?

   A. A. Being physically present only
   B. Appearing via a phone call
   C. Presence, physically or electronically, as required
   D. Sending a photo ID

39. A person named in a will to administer the estate of the deceased is called the:

   A. Executor
   B. Intestate
   C. Administrator
   D. Surrogate

40. Which of the following acts can a notary public do?

   A. Advertise his business
   B. Execute an acknowledgment of a will
   C. Give legal advice
   D. Draw up a deed

PRACTICE TEST 4: ANSWER KEY

1. **A. Common school education**
   Section 130 – Appointment of Notaries Public .... Page 5
2. **B. To confirm the validity of an identification credential**
   Section 182.6 – Credential Analysis .... Page 67
3. **C. $1**
   Section 132 – Certificates of official character of notaries public .... Page 9
4. **A. Be a United States citizen**
   Section 130 – Appointment of Notaries Public .... Page 5
5. **D. Notary services are free during normal business hours**
   Section 534 – County Law .... Page 13
6. **B. Verifying the identity of individuals**
   Section 182.2 – Definitions .... Page 59
7. **A. 18**
   Become a Notary Public in New York .... Page ii
8. **D. None of the above**
   Section 130 – Appointment of Notaries Public .... Page 5
9. **B. Attestation clause**
   Attestation clause .... Page 78
10. **A. Secure from interception**
    Section 135-c – Electronic Notarization .... Page 21
11. **D. $3**
    Section 133 – Certification of notarial signatures .... Page 10
12. **A. Attestation clause**
    Attestation clause .... Page 78
13. **C. Secretary of State**
    Section 130 – Appointment of Notaries Public .... Page 5
14. **A. $60**
    Section 182.11 – Fees .... Page 74
15. **D. An oath**
    Affirmation .... Page 77
16. **C. A third-party service provider approved by the notary**
    Section 182.6 – Credential Analysis .... Page 67
17. **B. Affidavit**
    Affidavit .... Page 77
18. **C. Administrator**
    Administrator .... Page 77
19. **B. Within 90 days before their commission expires**
    Section 182.10 – Applications, Registrations and Renewals .... Page 72
20. **B. Second**

Section 170.10 – Forgery in the second degree .... Page 54
21. A. An authentication certified for international use
    Apostile .... Page 78
22. C. The Secretary of State
    Member of Legislature .... Page 13
23. C. Personal appearance for the duration of the transaction
    Section 182.3 – Requirements for Notaries .... Page 62
24. D. All of the above
    Section 134 – Signature and seal of county clerk .... Page 17
25. D. None of the above
    Section 69 – Fee for administering certain official oaths prohibited .... Page 52
26. C. No, it cannot be deemed equivalent to an attestation clause
    Professional Conduct .... Page 1
27. B. A valid, current ID with photo, physical description, and signature
    Section 182.5 – Satisfactory Evidence of Identity .... Page 66
28. B. Misdemeanor
    Acknowledgment .... Page 77
29. B. They vacate their seat in the legislature
    Member of Legislature .... Page 13
30. B. Sheriff
    Sheriffs .... Page 14
31. B. Attestation of personal knowledge
    Section 182.5 – Satisfactory Evidence of Identity .... Page 66
32. A. Affiant saying "I do" or words of like meaning after the oath is read
    Oath .... Page 81
33. C. Secretary of State
    Section 132 – Certificates of official character of notaries public .... Page 9
34. B. Name, address, commission details, electronic technology description, and electronic signature exemplar
    Section 182.10 – Applications, Registrations and Renewals .... Page 72
35. A. A person found guilty of contempt of court
    Contempt of Court .... Page 79
36. B. Yes, if not satisfied with the principal's competency or signature voluntariness
    Section 135-c – Electronic Notarization .... Page 21
37. B. Chattel paper
    Chattel Paper .... Page 78
38. C. Presence, physically or electronically, as required
    Section 182.2 – Definitions .... Page 59
39. A. Executor
    Executor .... Page 80
40. A. Advertise his business
    Section 135-b – Advertising by notaries public .... Page 19

NEW YORK NOTARY PUBLIC STUDY GUIDE | 121

PRACTICE TEST 5: ANSWER SHEET

1. Ⓐ Ⓑ Ⓒ Ⓓ 11. Ⓐ Ⓑ Ⓒ Ⓓ 21. Ⓐ Ⓑ Ⓒ Ⓓ 31. Ⓐ Ⓑ Ⓒ Ⓓ

2. Ⓐ Ⓑ Ⓒ Ⓓ 12. Ⓐ Ⓑ Ⓒ Ⓓ 22. Ⓐ Ⓑ Ⓒ Ⓓ 32. Ⓐ Ⓑ Ⓒ Ⓓ

3. Ⓐ Ⓑ Ⓒ Ⓓ 13. Ⓐ Ⓑ Ⓒ Ⓓ 23. Ⓐ Ⓑ Ⓒ Ⓓ 33. Ⓐ Ⓑ Ⓒ Ⓓ

4. Ⓐ Ⓑ Ⓒ Ⓓ 14. Ⓐ Ⓑ Ⓒ Ⓓ 24. Ⓐ Ⓑ Ⓒ Ⓓ 34. Ⓐ Ⓑ Ⓒ Ⓓ

5. Ⓐ Ⓑ Ⓒ Ⓓ 15. Ⓐ Ⓑ Ⓒ Ⓓ 25. Ⓐ Ⓑ Ⓒ Ⓓ 35. Ⓐ Ⓑ Ⓒ Ⓓ

6. Ⓐ Ⓑ Ⓒ Ⓓ 16. Ⓐ Ⓑ Ⓒ Ⓓ 26. Ⓐ Ⓑ Ⓒ Ⓓ 36. Ⓐ Ⓑ Ⓒ Ⓓ

7. Ⓐ Ⓑ Ⓒ Ⓓ 17. Ⓐ Ⓑ Ⓒ Ⓓ 27. Ⓐ Ⓑ Ⓒ Ⓓ 37. Ⓐ Ⓑ Ⓒ Ⓓ

8. Ⓐ Ⓑ Ⓒ Ⓓ 18. Ⓐ Ⓑ Ⓒ Ⓓ 28. Ⓐ Ⓑ Ⓒ Ⓓ 38. Ⓐ Ⓑ Ⓒ Ⓓ

9. Ⓐ Ⓑ Ⓒ Ⓓ 19. Ⓐ Ⓑ Ⓒ Ⓓ 29. Ⓐ Ⓑ Ⓒ Ⓓ 39. Ⓐ Ⓑ Ⓒ Ⓓ

10. Ⓐ Ⓑ Ⓒ Ⓓ 20. Ⓐ Ⓑ Ⓒ Ⓓ 30. Ⓐ Ⓑ Ⓒ Ⓓ 40. Ⓐ Ⓑ Ⓒ Ⓓ

PRACTICE TEST 5

1. Who must be with a bank employee to witness the opening of a safe deposit box that has its lease terminated?

   A. A police officer or sheriff
   B. A bank officer or employee of the lessor
   C. The lessee
   D. A notary public

2. How long is the term for a notary public appointed and commissioned by the secretary of state?

   A. 2 years
   B. 4 years
   C. 6 years
   D. 10 years

3. Where does the jurisdiction of a New York State notary public extend throughout?

   A. United States
   B. New York State
   C. County of residence only
   D. City of residence only

4. What is required for a "Principal" in electronic notarization?

   A. Must be a New York resident
   B. Must be physically present in the notary's office
   C. Must sign the record electronically
   D. Must be a U.S. citizen

5. A notary public resides in Connecticut but has a business in NYS. Which of the following is he allowed to do?

   A. Administer oaths in NYS only
   B. Administer oaths in NYS and in Connecticut
   C. Give legal advice in NYS only
   D. None of the above

6. What is "Identity verification" in the context of notarization?

   A. Authenticating the identity of parties involved
   B. A formality with no real purpose
   C. Checking the notary's identity
   D. Verifying the notary's credentials

7. An acknowledgment should not be taken unless the notary public has satisfactory evidence that the person making the acknowledgment:

   A. Is the person described
   B. Has paid the $2 fee
   C. Is the person who executed the instrument
   D. A and C

8. What can replace the need for traditional identity verification methods in electronic notarization?

   A. A notary's personal attestation of knowing the individual
   B. A digital ID card only
   C. An email verification link
   D. A scanned copy of any ID

NEW YORK NOTARY PUBLIC STUDY GUIDE

9. Which of the following fees is a notary public allowed to ask for?

   A. A fee in advance before rendering any services
   B. A fee greater than is allowed
   C. A fee for any notary public services
   D. None of the above

10. How many current documents with the individual's signature are needed if not using an ID card?

    A. One
    B. Two
    C. Three
    D. None, if the notary knows them

11. Which of the following is not considered forgery in the second degree?

    A. Alters a public record with the intent to deceive
    B. Taking an acknowledgment before taking oath of office
    C. Completes a will with the intent to defraud
    D. Intends to injure another by falsely making a written instrument

12. Where can the guidelines for the required identity proofing standard be found?

    A. On the New York State Department of State website
    B. Through an online search engine only
    C. In the local library
    D. In the Digital Identity Guidelines by National Institute of Standards and Technology

13. What is the county clerk fee for a certificate of official character?

    A. $1
    B. $5
    C. $11
    D. It is a free service to the general public

14. How must electronic notaries verify a principal's location if outside the United States?

    A. By receiving a written statement
    B. The principal must provide a utility bill
    C. Using a GPS tracking device
    D. Through verbal confirmation during the notarial act

15. Which of the following statement is correct when a notary public is guilty of fraudulent practice?

    A. Liable in damages to the person injured
    B. Liable to an action to the person injured
    C. Liable for a fine up to $500
    D. Liable for a fine up to $1000

16. Which of the following is NOT allowed by a notary public in New York?

    A. Administering oaths in person
    B. Taking acknowledgments over the telephone
    C. Requiring the appearance of parties for notarization
    D. Refusing to execute a certificate unless identity is proved

17. What type of network must be used for performing an electronic notarial act?

    A. Public Wi-Fi
    B. A network with location detection
    C. A VPN network
    D. Any internet connection

18. Which of the follow are defects that will cause a notary public act to be deemed invalid?

    A. Expiration of his term
    B. Vacating of his office by change of his residence
    C. The action was taken outside his jurisdiction
    D. All of the above

19. How is an electronic record's integrity ensured during notarization?

    A. By attaching an electronic signature detectable for alterations
    B. Ignoring any changes to the document
    C. Using a password-protected PDF
    D. Through verbal agreement only

20. What is the minimum term of an indeterminate sentence for a class D felony?

    A. 3 years
    B. 4 years
    C. 7 years
    D. There is no minimum sentence

21. For how long must electronic notaries maintain audio-video conference recordings?

    A. 1 year
    B. 5 years
    C. 10 years
    D. Indefinitely

22. A law enacted by the New York State legislature is called:

    A. Codicil
    B. Seal
    C. Attestation
    D. Statute

23. What does the authenticity test for an ID credential include?

    A. Only a visual check of the photo
    B. Verification of physical and cryptographic security features
    C. An in-person interview
    D. A handwriting analysis

24. What must a notary public who is not a NYS attorney include if he advertises his services as a notary public in a foreign language?

    A. A disclaimer written in English that states he is not an attorney
    B. A disclaimer written in the same foreign language that states he is not an attorney
    C. The notary public services he provides
    D. None of the above

25. How does "Identity proofing" assist in electronic notarization?

    A. By providing legal advice

B. Validating and verifying personal information
   C. By proofreading documents
   D. Ensuring document integrity

26. Which of the following statements is correct when a notary public notarizes an affidavit?

   A. The notary public can negotiate a fee
   B. The notary public may charge a $3 fee
   C. The notary public must charge a $5 fee
   D. None of the above

27. What is the consequence for a notary's refusal to administer an oath or affidavit when requested?

   A. It is considered a misdemeanor
   B. There are no legal consequences
   C. It results in a warning for the first offense
   D. Immediate revocation of the notary's license

28. Which of the following is the section of an affidavit where the notary public certifies that it was sworn to before him?

   A. Jurat
   B. Swear
   C. Seal
   D. Affidavit

29. What does the remote online notarial certificate need to clearly state?

   A. That the act was performed using communication technology
   B. The notary's full name and address
   C. The principal's agreement to the terms
   D. The exact time the notarization took place

30. A notary public who is an attorney at law admitted to practice in NYS may:

   1. Administer an oath or affirmation
   2. Take the affidavit or acknowledgment of his client in respect of any matter

   A. 1 and 2 are not correct
   B. Only 1 is correct
   C. Only 2 is correct
   D. 1 and 2 are correct

31. What is "Public key infrastructure" related to in notarization?

   A. Building security for notary offices
   B. A cryptographic system for secure electronic signatures
   C. Infrastructure for public notary offices
   D. A public database of all notaries

32. What is the maximum jail sentence for a class D felony?

   A. 7 years
   B. 1 year
   C. 3 years
   D. There is no maximum sentence

33. How does the technology ensure the integrity of the electronic record presented for notarization?

   A. By comparing it to a physical copy
   B. Through blockchain verification

C. Ensuring it's the same record signed by the principal
D. By watermarking the document

34. What is a deponent?

    A. One named in a will to carry out the provisions
    B. The testimony of a witness taken out of court under oath/affirmation
    C. The agreement which creates or provides for the security interest
    D. A person who testifies to information or facts under oath in a deposition

35. What information must not be disclosed by the notary, except under specific conditions?

    A. The notary's personal address
    B. Access information for the notary's electronic signature
    C. The fee charged for notarization
    D. The names of principals served

36. What do applicants for reappointment of a notary public commission submit to the county clerk?

    A. Their application to the oath of office
    B. A $60 non-refundable application fee
    C. A "pass slip" showing that he has taken and passed the notary exam
    D. A and B

37. What does the communication technology need to include regarding record modification?

    A. Ability to edit records freely
    B. Process to add changes without tracking
    C. Reproduction process that tracks changes
    D. Unlimited deletions without record

38. When does an individual commit perjury?

    A. By forgetting details during testimony
    B. By making a false statement under oath knowingly and willfully
    C. By speaking without taking an oath
    D. By changing their testimony later

39. What consequence may a notary public in New York face for a third violation of the state's notary regulations?

    A. Mandatory retraining only
    B. A fine of exactly one thousand dollars
    C. Removal from office after a hearing
    D. Suspension for a minimum of one year

40. Who can administer oaths to corporation members?

    A. Only a notary public
    B. Any listed official who is part of the corporation
    C. Listed officials, excluding interested parties
    D. Exclusively external attorneys

PRACTICE TEST 5: ANSWER KEY

1. D. A notary public
   Section 335 – Banking Law .... Page 44
2. B. 4 years
   Section 182.10 – Applications, Registrations and Renewals .... Page 72
3. B. New York State
   Section 130 – Appointment of Notaries Public .... Page 5
4. C. Must sign the record electronically
   Section 135-c – Electronic Notarization .... Page 21
5. A. Administer oaths in NYS only
   Section 130 – Appointment of Notaries Public .... Page 5
6. A. Authenticating the identity of parties involved
   Section 182.2 – Definitions .... Page 59
7. D. A and C
   Section 303 – Requisites of acknowledgments .... Page 36
8. A. A notary's personal attestation of knowing the individual
   Section 182.5 – Satisfactory Evidence of Identity .... Page 66
9. A. A fee in advance before rendering any services
   Section 67 – Fees of public officers .... Page 51
10. B. Two
    Section 182.5 – Satisfactory Evidence of Identity .... Page 66
11. B. Taking an acknowledgment before taking oath of office
    Section 170.10 – Forgery in the second degree .... Page 54
12. D. In the Digital Identity Guidelines by National Institute of Standards and Technology
    Section 182.7 – Identity Proofing .... Page 69
13. A. $1
    Section 132 – Certificates of official character of notaries public .... Page 9
14. D. Through verbal confirmation during the notarial act
    Section 182.4 – Additional Requirements for Electronic Notaries .... Page 64
15. A. Liable in damages to the person injured
    Section 330 – Officers guilty of malfeasance liable for damages.................. Page 42
16. B. Taking acknowledgments over the telephone
    Professional Conduct .... Page 1
17. B. A network that allows location detection
    Section 182.4 – Additional Requirements for Electronic Notaries .... Page 64
18. D. All of the above
    Section 142-a – Validity of acts of notaries public .... Page 31
19. A. By attaching an electronic signature detectable for alterations
    Section 135-c – Electronic Notarization .... Page 21
20. A. 3 years

    Section 70.00 – Sentence of imprisonment for felony... Page 53
21. C. 10 years
    Section 135-c – Electronic Notarization .... Page 21
22. D. Statute
    Statute .... Page 82
23. B. Verification of physical and cryptographic security features
    Section 182.6 – Credential Analysis .... Page 68
24. B. A disclaimer written in the same foreign language that states he is not an attorney licensed to practice law
    Section 182.1 – Advertising... Page 58
25. B. Validating and verifying personal information
    Section 182.2 – Definitions .... Page 59
26. D. None of the above
    Acknowledgment .... Page 85
27. A. It is considered a misdemeanor
    Notary must officiate on request... Page 57
28. A. Jurat
    Jurat .... Page 80
29. A. That the act was performed using communication technology
    Section 182.4 – Additional Requirements for Electronic Notaries................................. Page 64
30. D. 1 and 2 are correct
    Section 135 – Powers and duties .... Page 17
31. B. A cryptographic system for secure electronic signatures
    Section 182.2 – Definitions .... Page 59
32. A. 7 years
    Section 70.00 – Sentence of imprisonment for felony... Page 53
33. C. Ensuring it's the same record signed by the principal
    Section 182.8 – Communication Technology .... Page 70
34. D. A person who testifies to information or facts under oath in a deposition
    Deponent... Page 79
35. B. Access information for the notary's electronic signature
    Section 182.4 – Additional Requirements for Electronic Notaries................................. Page 64
36. D. A and B
    Section 131 – Procedure of appointment; fees and commissions..................................... Page 7
37. C. Reproduction process that tracks changes
    Section 182.8 – Communication Technology .... Page 70
38. B. By making a false statement under oath knowingly and willfully
    Perjury... Page 57
39. C. Removal from office after a hearing
    Section 135-b – Advertising by notaries public... Page 19
40. C. Listed officials, excluding interested parties
    Section 138 – Powers of notaries public or other officers .... Page 30

TRUE OR FALSE: ANSWER KEY

1. FALSE
   The New York Secretary of State mandates that notaries must not take acknowledgments or affidavits without the physical presence of the person involved
2. FALSE
   A notary public vacates their position once they move out of the state and holds no place of business within NYS
3. FALSE
   A $10 fee will be requested for a duplicate card
4. TRUE
   This is permitted for a fee of $1
5. TRUE
   For a fee of $3, a county clerk will verify the certificate
6. FALSE
   Once removed, notaries public are no longer eligible to be a notary public
7. TRUE
   An inspector of elections is eligible to become a notary public
8. TRUE
   Violation of the selective service draft act or its amendments bars eligibility for the office of notary public
9. FALSE
   Staff members of a county clerk appointed to become notaries public are exempt from examination and application fees
10. FALSE
    A member of the legislature must vacate their seat if they accept any paid civil office under the state government, however, they can keep their legislative seat if appointed to an uncompensated position, such as a notary public
11. FALSE
    A notary public is disqualified from acting in cases where they have a direct financial or beneficial interest in the transaction
12. FALSE
    The seal of a county clerk on an official character certificate of a notary public can be facsimile, printed, stamped, photographed, or engraved
13. TRUE
    Section 135 grants the power for notaries public to take affidavits and depositions in NYS
14. FALSE
    A notary public committing fraud is considered a misdemeanor, not a felony
15. FALSE

A notary public who is also an attorney may advertise their legal services in foreign languages
16. TRUE
A notary public has the discretion to refuse performing an electronic notarial act if they have doubts about the principal's competence or if the signature is not made voluntarily
17. TRUE
$2 is the amount authorized to charge for an oath or affirmation and an additional $2 for each additional person
18. FALSE
An attorney may write "Attorney and Counselor at Law" under his signature
19. TRUE
It is permitted that a notary public who is a stockholder of a company may take proof to a written instrument executed to that company
20. FALSE
A person cannot file a claim for defect if the defect was known about upon when it occurred. This is prevented by subdivision 3 of section 142-a
21. FALSE
Leases for less than 3 years are not conveyances
22. TRUE
A notary public is permitted to certify a conveyance at any place within the state
23. TRUE
Married women and unmarried women have the same rights in conveyances
24. FALSE
A notary public must know or have evidence that the person taking the acknowledgment is the person it describes
25. TRUE
A subscribing witness is required to certify that he knows the person signing the conveyance
26. FALSE
A notary public also must include the addresses of any subscribing witnesses
27. FALSE
Information required under section 300 is still needed
28. FALSE
The inclusion of the location within a proof of acknowledgment is viewed as a non-substantial variance
29. TRUE
A notary public is liable for damages to an injured party for fraud or malfeasance
30. FALSE
Conveyances must be in English, or have an authenticated translation
31. FALSE
The letter must be sent within 10 days
32. TRUE

It is within the power of a notary public to take depositions in a civil proceeding
33. FALSE
It is not within the power of a notary public to take the acknowledgment for witnesses of a marriage
34. TRUE
It is within the power of a notary public to administer the oath of a public officer
35. FALSE
A law student can work under the supervision of an appellate court approved legal aid organization after 2 semesters
36. FALSE
Violation of section 484 is a misdemeanor
37. TRUE
The supreme court has the power to punish individuals for unlawful practice of law
38. TRUE
It is legal to draft legal documents if the notary public is not a lawyer, as long as he has not made it a business to practice law and offer his services as an attorney at law
39. TRUE
A notary public is allowed to perform any duties of a notary public same day his oath of office has been taken and filed
40. TRUE
If the law allows it, a public offer can demand a fee before a duty is performed as stated by subdivision 3 of section 67
41. FALSE
No fee can be collected from any public employee, including a member of the legislature, for performing an oath of office
42. FALSE
A notary public that has knowingly made a false statement is guilty of a misdemeanor
43. FALSE
Class D felony can extend to 7 years
44. TRUE
1 year is the limit for misdemeanor violations
45. FALSE
Forgery is a class D felony
46. TRUE
Issuing a false certificate is a class E felony
47. FALSE
Official misconduct is a class A misdemeanor
48. TRUE
Refusing to perform notarization when requested is a misdemeanor for a notary public
49. FALSE
Perjury specifically involves knowingly making a false statement under oath or affirmation

50. FALSE

    Only when advertising in a foreign language other than English is it required to include a disclaimer on the advertisement

51. FALSE

    "Electronic notarial act" states that the notary public must be physically present in the state of New York at the time of the act

52. TRUE

    A notary public must inform the Secretary of State of any changes to their name, address, or email within five days, providing their official signature

53. FALSE

    A notary public must use a reliable electronic signature that is unique to them, securely attached to the electronic record, retained under their sole control, and linked to the data in a way that any changes to the record are detectable.

54. FALSE

    Even if an electronic notary public personally knows the individual, all other requirements for identity verification must still be met for the notarial act to be valid.

55. TRUE

    Credential analysis involves using technology to confirm the integrity of the ID's security features and information from the issuing or an authoritative source to ensure the validity of the ID details

56. FALSE

    Identity proofing must meet or exceed the Identity Assurance Level 2 standard set by the National Institute of Standards and Technology

57. TRUE

    The technology must include a process that records any changes, ensuring that additions, deletions, or alterations are traceable

58. FALSE

    A notary public is required to retain the notarization records for a minimum of ten years.

59. TRUE

    When registering the capability to perform electronic notarizations, notaries must provide an exemplar of their electronic signature using the system required by the secretary of state

60. FALSE

    The fee for each electronic notarial act performed by an electronic notary public is fixed at $25, inclusive of all costs.

Made in United States
Cleveland, OH
06 May 2025

16678262R00077